SHED DECOR

jacqui
small

SHED DECOR

HOW TO DECORATE & FURNISH YOUR FAVOURITE GARDEN ROOM

SALLY COULTHARD

First published in 2015 by
Jacqui Small LLP
An imprint of Aurum Press
74-77 White Lion Street
London N1 9PF

Publisher **Jacqui Small**
Managing Editor **Lydia Halliday**
Senior Editor **Claire Chandler**
Designer **Helen Bratby**
Picture Editor **Caroline Rowland**
Editor **Sian Parkhouse**
Production **Maeve Healy**

ISBN: 978 1 909342 80 4
A catalogue record for this book
is available from the British Library.

2018 2017 2016
10 9 8 7 6 5 4 3 2 1

Printed in China

CONTENTS

9 Introduction

13 Part 1: Shed Decor Styles
16 The Rustic Shed
36 The Vintage Shed
58 The Plain & Simple Shed
80 The Recycled Shed
102 The Retro Shed
120 The Country Shed

141 Part 2: Shed Decor Basics
144 Approaches to Shed Space
148 Walls
152 Flooring
158 Heat & Power
166 Fabric
174 Furniture
186 Storage

202 Directory
204 Index
207 Picture Credits

SHEDS – where else can you carve out a space that's completely and utterly your own, decorate it as you please and lock yourself away for hours, pursuing your favourite pastime, whether it's tinkering with a classic motorbike or throwing paint at a canvas?

There's something really important about creating a space in your life that allows you to be yourself. So many of our waking hours are spent doing things for other people – work, commuting, family life, domestic chores. That's not to say we don't enjoy all the comforting, familiar chaos of daily life, but it's also crucial to save something for yourself. Sheds give us the freedom and permission to do something that's life-affirming, creative or just really good fun.

I can hardly believe it's been several years since *Shed Chic* came out. I don't think the publishers or I really had an idea just how positive the response would be, and of the many books I've written it's been the one people ask me about most. *Shed Chic* took a whistle-stop tour of all the different types of sheds, huts and cabins currently on the market, and encouraged readers to think about the different uses sheds could be put to; from home offices to playrooms, extra bedrooms to creative studios, the options were myriad and inspiring. And while *Shed Chic* was a book mostly about shed design and function, it's time to fling open the doors and step into shed interiors.

So welcome to *Shed Decor*, a book dedicated to decorating and equipping your shed space for relaxing, working and playing. From unpromising potting sheds to tired old summerhouses, *Shed Decor* will show you how, with the right combination of

The ultimate retreat (opposite) What could be cosier than a sleeping shack, tucked away among the trees and flowers? Free from the distractions of daily life, this rustic cabin is perfect for guest rests or your very own backyard adventure.

Small space, big ideas Compact living doesn't have to be cramped. This elegant hideaway (right) combines a space-saving wood burner, white paintwork and carefully chosen accessories to create a light and breezy home from home. The interior of whitewashed timber is sparse but welcoming (opposite). Dark accents, bold oversized artwork and simple fabrics add warmth and contrast to an otherwise bleached palette.

colours, fabrics, furniture and accessories, anyone can transform an outdoor building into a favourite garden room. Whether you want a rustic hideaway or an urban den, a 'salvage chic' shoffice or a quirky creative hub, you'll find hundreds of bright ideas, how-to guides and interior designer 'tricks' to quickly and inexpensively create a cosy and inviting space. Most importantly, you'll see that shed decoration allows you to express yourself in ways above and beyond the constraints of your own home. When a den is completely yours, you can indulge every design whim. When a space is small, your budget goes a long way. And when you don't have to share it with anyone else, that little hut at the bottom of the garden becomes a place more precious than money can ever buy.

SHED DECOR STYLES

Part 1 of this book takes a tour of six of the most popular shed styles – Rustic, Vintage, Plain & Simple, Recycled, Retro and Country – and outlines the key design elements that go into each of these distinctive decors. And this isn't a book just for looking – at every stage there are top tips, get-the-look guides and easy instructions to help you along the way. This section also takes a sneaky peek at some of the world's most delectable hideaways, from rugged American huts and artisan retreats to stylish Scandinavian sheds.

RUSTIC

VINTAGE

PLAIN & SIMPLE

RECYCLED

RETRO

COUNTRY

THE RUSTIC SHED

Back to basics (opposite) Rough, unfinished timber and naive furniture blend beautifully with homespun fabrics and feminine accents to create a timeless pioneer aesthetic. Hides, blankets and cushions bring a textural interest and a touch of home comfort.

Wood as wallpaper (overleaf, left) Timber has its own rich and varied colour palette. Even within one single length of wood, you'll find gently changing hints and tones, natural patination and acres of visual and textural interest. (overleaf, right) Children instinctively understand the pleasure of a rustic hideaway, surrounded by nature and organic textures. This tree house is wonderfully makeshift and offers its residents a chance to spend precious time outdoors without the possibility of rain spoiling play.

One of the delights of working in a shed is your connection to nature. There are few things more pleasurable than time spent tucked in a garden hideaway, protected from the elements and surrounded by the sights, sounds and smells of nature in all its glory. Time seems to collapse, you lose hours as you potter around the shed, tending to seedlings or absorbed in a creative pursuit.

Dressing down (right) Keep accessories to a minimum in a rustic interior. Animal skins, a mirror framed with antlers and a hoop-and-stave wooden keg – these low-key but carefully chosen accents bring this log cabin to life.

Bucolic bathroom (below) An enamel bowl perched on top of a battered wooden trunk together make a glorious washstand, while sheep horns provide witty but practical towel hangers.

Rustic with a twist (opposite) Don't feel confined to a certain look. This shed mixes key pieces of the rustic vocabulary – bare timber, chicken wire and battered furniture – with an oversized peacock lampshade and a Moroccan pierced-work lantern to create a quirky, one-off style.

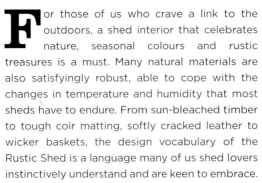

For those of us who crave a link to the outdoors, a shed interior that celebrates nature, seasonal colours and rustic treasures is a must. Many natural materials are also satisfyingly robust, able to cope with the changes in temperature and humidity that most sheds have to endure. From sun-bleached timber to tough coir matting, softly cracked leather to wicker baskets, the design vocabulary of the Rustic Shed is a language many of us shed lovers instinctively understand and are keen to embrace.

The rustic look is, at its heart, a relaxed, unaffected style, but that doesn't mean it's always easy to create. Natural materials such as wood or coir are often plain or roughly textured, and it can be a challenge to create a space that also feels warm and comfortable if we rely too heavily on such pragmatic materials. The key to a comfortable rustic look is to combine rough-tough elements with softer, more forgiving textures, such as linens and wools, as well as adding the odd splashes of colour to lift an otherwise bland palette.

We get so used to the infinite patterns and bright colours of modern fabrics that we sometimes forget the sheer elegance and beauty of natural fabrics in their rawest state. From the speckled

loveliness of unbleached cotton to the biscuity shades of hessian, natural fabrics are absolutely central to the Rustic Shed. Thanks to the lack of processing they need, they are also often cheaper than their manufactured counterparts and more forgiving of the stains and marks that come with a life lived outdoors.

The rustic look is also a deeply practical interior scheme for a shed, especially one that's going to be used for gardening, messy creative pursuits or outdoor play. For these kinds of activities you're going to need furniture, finishes and fabrics that can take a hammering. Scuffed timber work surfaces, hessian seat covers and tough storage options, such as wooden crates or woven boxes, will cope with the demands of practical activities.

Seating and tables need to withstand muddy wellies, soil-splattered trousers and the occasional downpour when we've forgotten to bring the furniture inside. Chairs designed to sit outside throughout the year are suited to this tough existence – metal bistro chairs, for example, whether salvaged or brand new, are relatively inexpensive, hardy and light enough to store folded away on your shed wall if floor space is tight.

One of the keys to rustic chic is the blurring of boundaries between indoors and out. Stealing ideas from the garden and dragging them into your shed is a sure-fire way to add a refreshing outdoorsy vibe. Terracotta pots and planters work as brilliantly inside the shed as they do in the garden – use them as storage pots, shelf dividers, cut-flower vases or upside down as coffee-table legs. Fill them with pens, plant markers and other tools of the trade, plant them up with fragrant herbs and place on a sunny surface, or create an eye-catching display using reclaimed pots with unusual makers' names or patinas. Other accessories that sit comfortably in this robust aesthetic include well-loved watering cans, *objets trouvés* and gardening tools as decorative wall art.

When it comes to colour schemes, let the materials do the talking. Timber comes in an almost infinite

array of delicate shades, from the creamy whiteness of ash to dark and brooding tropical hardwoods such as bubinga. Don't be afraid to mix up wood colours – different types of timber have a pleasing way of visually 'getting on', and you'll get some nice tonal variations even within the same species. One note of caution, however. Outdoor timber, especially if it's on the less expensive side, is often stained with cheap preservatives. While these chemicals will certainly lengthen the life of your shed, they have the unfortunate effect of giving timber an unnatural orange or greenish tinge. Don't be afraid to restain these woods a different darker shade, or cover with a diluted wash of exterior paint.

Settler chic (opposite) The soft, distressed paint colours, timber backdrop and simple, handcrafted furniture all add up to a gentle, nostalgic 'settler aesthetic'. Undyed linen, antique accents and plain woven rugs contribute to the feel.

The bare essentials (above) The antithesis of a modern fitted kitchen, this elegantly functional food preparation area provides the bare essentials for rustling up a rustic meal. The scrubbed-pine table, plate rack and hanging storage hit just the right note.

A touch of glamour (above left) Rustic but sophisticated, this log cabin is lifted to another level with exquisite antique touches – a pair of elaborate wall sconces, a rich red runner and an elegant hall table complete the look.

Statement pieces (right) Rustic Shed decor suits fewer, larger pieces of furniture, rather than a dainty collection. This antique free-standing cupboard makes a strong, masculine statement and holds its own in imposing surroundings.

Coastal charm (below) There's something of the sea in this refined take on rustic – the sailing accessories, marine blues and dazzling whites create a relaxed, breezy interior. Rough timber walls stop the scheme feeling too 'beach holiday hut'.

Wools, linens and other natural, undyed fabrics look at home in a Rustic Shed, but to break up the monotony of a neutral colour palette try to introduce different textures to create interest. Chunky wool knitted throws, crisp cotton canvas, hides and naturally coloured leathers will blend beautifully and add a touchy-feely counterpoint to rough sawn timbers and woven rugs. Add colour in judicious splashes or stick to a naturally inspired palette – artificially bright shades such as acid yellow and neon tones will tend to dominate this subtle palette, so use bright pops of colour only in small amounts.

In the Rustic Shed, accessories have to work hard to earn their inclusion. Things have to be beautiful and useful if they want to fit in; this isn't the scheme for glamorous, shiny trinkets or plush fabrics. Think galvanized buckets, peg rails and storage crates. Tough outdoor materials, such as wicker and rattan, are cheap to buy, sustainable and surprisingly robust, making them ideal for storage and the perfect accessory in a Rustic Shed. Smaller woven baskets with lids double as excellent storage pots for stationery and craft supplies, while larger bins and hampers will tidy away all manner of tools and equipment.

Lighting is unfussy, practical and task-focused. Anglepoise lamps, bare pendant light bulbs or basic clip-on spotlights create the right look, while candles and storm lanterns can soften the atmosphere as the night draws in.

Rustic and restful (opposite) If you want to create a rustic but relaxing space, try to soften the look with a few decadent touches. In this sleep space, the rough-tough accessories – horns, rusted iron lanterns and sack-cloth pillows – are balanced by the silky velvet cushion and vintage eiderdown.

ESSENTIALS

SHED STYLE NOTES: **RUSTIC**

Mix and match tough textures and soft, **natural** fabrics. For gentle colour and feel-appeal, think **rough timber**, raw **linen** and unbleached cottons. Add hard-working, practical accessories – **zinc** planters, **wicker** baskets and **wooden** crates – and bring warmth and cosiness with chunky **wool** throws, **sheepskins** and a roaring woodstove **fire**.

WICKER BASKETS ARE PERFECT FOR STACKED LOGS, ROLLED BLANKETS AND FAVOURITE MAGAZINES

COARSE-TEXTURED, NATURAL FIBRE FLOORING. SUSTAINABLE AND HARD-WEARING

ALL-WEATHER CAFE TABLES AND CHAIRS ARE BOTH PRACTICAL AND PRETTY

RUGGED WOOL SOFTNESS. USE AS A THROW OR FOR COMFORT UNDERFOOT

HUNTING HUT

We've all grown up with the idea of a log cabin deep in the woods. It's not difficult to close your eyes and imagine the sounds and smells of forest life – the smoking campfire, resinous trees and dawn chorus. It's the stuff of childhood adventures – packing up a rucksack and stumbling upon a secret hideaway – and this little rustic hut in the middle of Sweden's Svartadalen forest has more than a touch of Hansel and Gretel about it.

But don't be fooled. This isn't a pastiche of some rural retreat. It's a living, breathing, working hut, built more than thirty years ago and still used as a resting point for hunters on the trail of deer and elk. As with many log cabins, the choice of materials and decor is dictated by practicality not fashion. Out here in the Swedish wilderness, any furniture and fittings have to be carried from the nearest road, so it makes sense to construct as much as possible from your immediate surroundings. Almost everything in the hut was made using wood felled from the pine forest. From the outdoor benches to the pot hooks and peg rails, each piece is cut, carved and whittled from what's to hand. The walls, floors and ceiling are, of course, timber, but it's hard not to admire the ingenuity of someone who can also create seating, tables, cupboards, chopping boards, hanging hooks, stools, tools, shelves and even door handles from the same simple material.

Warmth and shelter (left) A small wood-burning stove kicks out companionable warmth in this tiny hunting hut. Firewood is kept neatly stowed under the handmade storage cupboard, while peg rails and hooks keep all the essentials out of harm's way.
Fireside stories (opposite) Simple, handcrafted benches circle the open campfire, perfect for sitting and telling tales after the sun's gone down. Almost everything in this idyllic spot was cut and carved from local forest timber.

To add comfort and warmth, a small cast-iron stove fills the hut with radiant heat; while a vintage paraffin lantern and candlesticks create an instant, portable glow. Only a few pots and pans are needed – a simple traditional Swedish kettle and basic tools for housekeeping. It's a tough existence – there's no place for precious antiques or valuables in such a practical space, and even the tea is served in cheap and cheerful mid-century crockery. Decoration is refreshingly sparse, but no less beautiful for it. A simple glass bottle holds a handful of pine sprigs, while outside the hut is decorated with mossy antlers and plant wreaths.

But rustic doesn't have to mean cold and inhospitable. There's a Danish word, *hygge* – it's almost impossible to define but absolutely embodies the spirit of this shed. It's about building a sanctuary, a place of closeness, warmth and connection to the things that matter in life – nature, family, home, community. From sharing a meal with friends to sitting in front of a roaring fire, *hygge* is about living in the present and enjoying those small, comforting rituals in life that fulfil our basic needs but mean so very much. Technology and our fast-paced schedules often strip the pleasure from these everyday tasks, so it's refreshing to see a hut that's all about the simple things in life.

This is a hut that welcomes. From the gentle glow of candlelight to the warm colour of natural timber, it's a space that evokes comfort and conviviality. The face-to-face bench-seats at the table under the window inspire sociable meals and conversation, while the outdoor benches and roaring fire are perfect for summer evenings spent storytelling. And perhaps the most welcoming thing of all: when the owners aren't visiting they leave the hut open, as a place of sanctuary and warmth for passers-by who might have lost their way. Perhaps thoughts of Hansel and Gretel aren't so far off the mark after all.

A handful of home comforts (opposite, clockwise from top left) The gentle flicker and glow of candlelight invites passers-by to seek shelter; a vintage Swedish kettle sits with second-hand candlesticks; handcrafted hooks keep chopping boards and pans safely stowed; a traditional Swedish sweeping brush and a 1950s stool add a touch of nostalgia.
Space-saving ideas (right) With limited floor space, built-in benches and a slim table create an ample eating area without compromising on comfort.

TREE HOUSE & TOOL SHED

Jon Carloftis is good at lots of things. He's a garden designer, author, business owner and TV presenter. But, perhaps most exciting of all, he's also a dab hand with sheds, managing to sneak not one but two beautifully crafted hideaways into his delightful Bucks County, Pennsylvania garden.

Being a master of small spaces and rooftop horticulture, it's perhaps not surprising that Jon could see the possibilities for outdoor buildings even in this relatively modest back garden. Sheds can take up precious gardening space, but by thinking vertically as well as horizontally, he was able to create a enviably chic treehouse and keep the original large tool shed, without making the outside green space feel cramped.

The treehouse is simple but exquisite. With help from a carpenter, Jon designed and constructed this elevated retreat from wide planks of pine and cedar wood, and salvaged doors and windows. Plucky visitors must scale a 4.5m (15-feet) rustic ladder to gain entry for a sleepover, while supplies are hoisted aboard with a makeshift pulley-and-crate system. It's also a garden building of contrasts – deliciously dark on the exterior, opening up into a light, whitewashed interior. Inside the space is dressed simply – just an antique iron bed for guests, neutral biscuit-shaded linens, a vintage stag's head, fishing tackle and a handful of *objets trouvés* plucked from around the garden. It's a style that mirrors the interior of Jon's gracious 1850s farmhouse – a space full of white walls into which he mixes fine antiques, salvaged treasures and witty accents.

Treetop dreaming (opposite) There are few ideas more rustic and romantic than a treetop bedroom, complete with ornate iron bed, luxurious throws and chunky knit cushions.
The boy scout spirit (above right) Intrepid guests need a head for heights and must scale a two-storey home-made ladder to gain entry to their quarters. (right) Supplies are transported up and down thanks to an ingenious crate-and-pulley system.

Safely back on ground you'll find Jon's tool shed, which also doubles as a winter garage for his 1952 Cadillac. Built in the 1920s, it's seen little alteration over the years apart from a new floor of loosely laid Carrara marble. From the wooden rafters hang iron lanterns, reclaimed from a Kentucky church but more than at home in their new secular setting, while a naive timber table makes a striking centrepiece and useful working surface.

Tool sheds can be tricky to get right. For anyone with an ounce of aesthetics, there can be a real battle between creating a good-looking space and one that functions as a useful store. It's possible you get as much pleasure from seeing stacked terracotta pots and watering cans in a row as you do from growing and tending to your plants. You might be desperate to display your gardenalia and vintage tools, but don't want to stumble over them every time you step through the door.

But there's a solution. Thinking vertically again, Jon makes the most of the tool shed's walls, hanging rakes, trowels and spades safely out of harm's way but still within easy reach. Small terracotta pots are stacked on any free vertical struts, while piled on the floor you find galvanized containers, wooden crates and traditional clay planters. It's a glorious collection of garden implements and, for any enthusiast, art in its own right. Wooden fruit crates are put to use here too – this time as handy storage units, displaying a team of horsey ornaments, amateur paintings and other quirky finds.

It's a space that's both used and useful. Jon's client list might be stellar but his garden philosophy is refreshingly down-to-earth. It's an approach that celebrates nature, rather than tries to control it, embraces natural materials rather than hard, urban textures. It's the embodiment of everything a Rustic Shed should be – joyous, unaffected and just that little bit wild.

Rustic reinvention (left) Wooden fruit crates are stacked to form a repurposed shelving unit, ideal for Jon's quirky horse-themed ornaments and paintings.

Tools of the trade (opposite) Vintage garden tools make an arresting statement displayed en masse. The hanging lanterns, which came from an old church, are comfortably rehomed in this delightfully organized working space.

THE VINTAGE SHED

Faded glory (opposite) The essence of vintage style is a romantic attachment to the past, seeing beauty and meaning in everyday items from times gone by. From heirloom fabrics to distressed furniture, old woven baskets to mismatched crockery, vintage has to be the homeliest of all the styles.

Beside the seaside (overleaf, left) You can't get much more nostalgic than a vintage beach hut. This spirit-lifting seaside retreat invokes memories of British summer holidays, with its 1950s blue-and-white paint scheme and lollipop splashes of colour.

Simple pleasures (overleaf, right) Vintage doesn't have to equate with clutter. This delightful bedroom takes a restrained approach, with just a few eye-catching pieces set against a white, beach hut background. The floral lampshade, tartan throw and stacked paperbacks are perfect props.

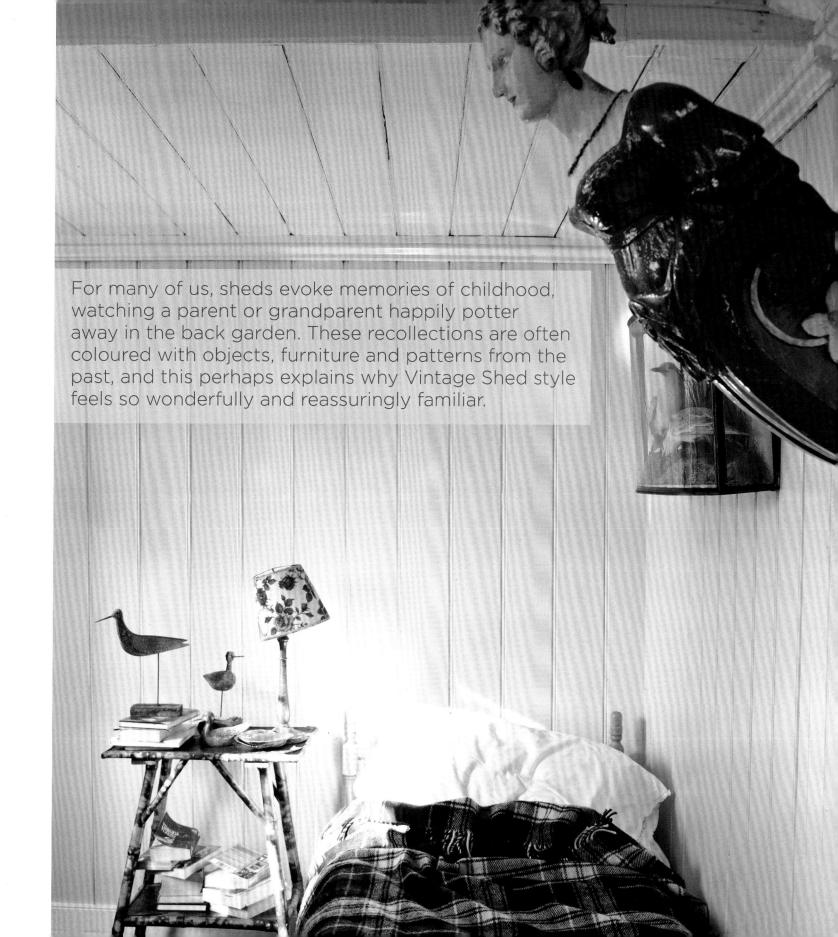

For many of us, sheds evoke memories of childhood, watching a parent or grandparent happily potter away in the back garden. These recollections are often coloured with objects, furniture and patterns from the past, and this perhaps explains why Vintage Shed style feels so wonderfully and reassuringly familiar.

Vintage as a trend has permeated almost every corner of home design, so it's no surprise that it should have made its way into garden buildings. Unlike antiques, which can often seem stuffy or intimidating, the appeal of vintage is in its accessibility and kitsch good humour. From homespun crochet throws to blousy prints, battered old furniture to pretty kitchenalia, sheds can look fantastic filled with vintage reminiscences and reminders.

Often inexpensive and very easy to source at fleamarkets and junk shops, vintage pieces are also a quick way to add character and personality to a shed space. Vintage furniture and accessories aren't just decorative, they also have the power to add charm and a sense of nostalgia to an outdoor building. The term 'vintage' usually describes items more than two decades old but less than one hundred – so most pieces come from time periods we can remember or from only a few generations back. This makes vintage, of all the decorative styles, perhaps the most cosy and homely, drawing on comforting feelings of childhood and the lovely ordinariness of family life.

As a style, vintage covers a huge variety of 'looks' from the shabby sophistication of French château chic to the British interpretation with its china tea cups, rosebud fabrics and cheerful make-do-and-mend ethics. Vintage has other faces too – folksy, wartime, faded glory, boudoir and many more. All vintage styles, however, share common threads. These include finding beauty in everyday objects, loving all things battered, bumped and distressed, and embracing the home-made and homespun.

One of the criticisms levelled at vintage style is that it can sometimes tip over into being twee. This often happens if we try too hard to create the vintage look straight from the high street. Modern reproductions of vintage patterns and products are fantastically accessible and an instant resource to draw on, but they have to be watered down with original pieces to stave off the shop-bought look. There's no substitute for trudging around car-boot sales and charity shops, picking up knick-knacks and one-off treasures – only then will you create a shed interior that's truly original and unique. It'll also save you a fortune in the long run, as most vintage decor is still very reasonably priced.

Joyful exuberance (opposite) In this resolutely cheerful take on vintage chic, bright pops of colour, childlike motifs and gleefully clashing patterns create a shed with real spirit; the neat organization and careful storage stop it from feeling chaotic.

Vintage on wheels (opposite and left) A gentle interpretation of vintage style, this shepherd's hut is filled with soft fifties colours – cornflower blues and pinks – and homely accessories. Vintage animal prints and blousy floral fabrics add the perfect farmhouse note. Fifties colour schemes were often deliberately over-coordinated – the pale blue colour scheme is carried through to the exterior shutters, door frame and steps. Even the deckchairs are painted to match.

It's also important to be true to your own interests and personality. Vintage style is all about the clutter and collections, but it has to be stuff that reflects who you are. If you're not interested in floral teacups and doilies, forget the bunting and create a vintage look with a different twist – sixties Americana, the Oxford don library-look, boutique chic, cocktail hour, old fishing paraphenalia ... there are plenty of different versions of vintage.

When it comes to filling your shed with vintage, a word of caution. Don't opt for expensive pieces. Unless you are lucky enough to have an outdoor building with the same security arrangements, heating and insulation as your home, anything valuable will struggle with shed conditions. Veneered furniture will peel if it's left in a damp environment, and vintage fabrics, quilts and upholstery may become mouldy, so stick to robust pieces or bring your decor indoors for winter.

One of the challenges when creating a Vintage Shed interior is how to build a cohesive look from a rag-tag collection of fleamarket finds and hand-me-downs. 'Eclectic' is a horribly overused word in interior design – there's no such thing as simply throwing together a random collection of furniture and fabrics and it looking instantly stylish; there's always editing and arranging to do. The vintage look is often a matter of trial and error, but follow these golden rules and you can't go far wrong:

Don't be afraid of pattern. Pile it on. Floral fabrics, however disparate, will harmonize if there's enough of them together. Flower patterns can be teamed with ticking and checks for the folksy vintage look.

Embrace the bumps and scratches. Distressed is good. It suggests a well-lived life and a story to tell. The odd repainted piece will brighten the look, but over-restored furniture can look soulless.

Close quarters (above) A mezzanine sleeping deck creates a cosy bed space without compromising the floor area. Soft, loosely covered furnishings complete the relaxed, rural look.

A space for play (right) A child's shed should be a place where they can relax, laugh and be themselves. Vintage decor is perfect as not only is most of it inexpensive and readily available, it also doesn't matter about the odd bump or scratch.

Thinking outside (below) You can carry the vintage theme through to the exterior of your shed, decorating it with collectible enamel signs, reclaimed lighting or old advertisements.

Personal treasures (opposite) The process of collecting and displaying personal mementos, fleamarket finds and bygone artefacts means no two sheds will ever be the same.

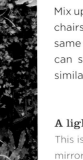

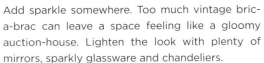

Add sparkle somewhere. Too much vintage bric-a-brac can leave a space feeling like a gloomy auction-house. Lighten the look with plenty of mirrors, sparkly glassware and chandeliers.

Have a collection. Vintage is a style that suits the collector. Adorn your shed with your very own vignette, whether it's Cornishware, a shelf of decorative biscuit tins or a wall plastered with vintage posters. There's beauty in numbers.

Mix up the eras. A table surrounded by mismatched chairs or a selection of kitsch paintings with the same subject – pieces from different decades can sit nicely together. Look for style or colour similarities to create a sense of cohesion.

Don't create a pastiche. Vintage style is all about creative clutter and glorious clashes. There needs to be a sense that the space has evolved over time. If you try too hard to recreate a particular era, it can start to feel like a living museum.

Have something home-made. Whether it's your granny's quilt or a handcrafted blanket, craft and creativity are key elements of vintage style. Sketches, naive paintings, decorated furniture, folk sculpture, handwritten signs – all add to the mix.

A lighter touch (overleaf, left) Vintage isn't always armfuls of clutter and clashing colours. This is a pared-back take on the romantic French château look; generous swathes of linen, an ornate mirror and touches of Provence blue nail the look.

Colour balance (overleaf, right) Even if you do display your favourite trinkets and treasures, keeping the colour palette limited creates a united, pleasing display. Here, whites, off-whites and blues provide all the colour needed, apart from cleverly chosen dots of carrot orange and orchid pink.

-Fetch Figs
-Anouk at 5.
-Make Brioche
- Honey *

ESSENTIALS

SHED STYLE NOTES: **VINTAGE**
Embrace all things handmade and
homespun – from **crochet** blankets
to heirloom **quilts**. Create **collections**
of everyday objects – kitchenalia,
old advertising signs or childhood
toys. Look for **fleamarket** furniture,
mismatched cushions and blousy,
nostalgic fabrics. Add **sparkle** with
mirrors and chandeliers. And don't be
afraid to pile on the **pattern**.

CROCHET THROWS ARE
A COSY WAY TO ADD
TEXTURE, HOMELY
CHARACTER AND
HANDMADE WARMTH

COLLECTIBLE TINS — NOSTALGIC,
COLOURFUL AND THE IDEAL
CONTAINER FOR SMALL STORAGE

STACKED SUITCASES CAN CREATE INSTANT SIDE TABLES OR PLENTIFUL STORAGE. ARRANGE IN SIZE ORDER

ADD BRIGHT POPS OF COLOUR OR FADED, DISTRESSED PIECES FOR INSTANT PERIOD CHARM

The Danes do minimalist sheds so well and it's hard not to feel a slight twinge of envy when we see yet another gorgeously pared-back summerhouse filled with a sprinkling of chic accessories. It's a clean, designer-led look that makes us consider our own decor and think perhaps it's time for a radical clear-out.

And yet, when it really comes down to it, just how cosy and comfortable is a space that echoes with its lack of furnishings and hard metallic accents? Our living spaces are supposed to reflect who we are – all the personal mementos, photos and knick-knacks say something meaningful about our life, loves and passions. Our favourite things – whether it's a tatty old cushion or a faded photograph – not only make fantastic decorations but they also bolster our sense of self and remind us who we are.

It's refreshing, then, to find a Danish summerhouse with an old-fashioned twist. This homely shed has managed to combine some of the must-have aesthetics of Scandinavian shed decor – black timber exterior, pure white interior – with just the right amount of personal, vintage treasures. As always, the all-white background provides a good starting point – the blank canvas of white tongue-and-groove walls stops the space feeling cluttered. But here things get interesting. Just a subtle change in tone – to a light blue/grey paint – is used to highlight the rafters and supporting posts, a colour carried through the summerhouse and onto the bedroom cupboards. This two-tone effect shouts 1950s beach holiday and gives the space an instant vintage vibe.

A trick of the eye (opposite) A cluttered floor space can make a shed feel cramped. Here, the owners have cleverly put most of the visual interest on the walls. Paintings, mirrors, sconces, lamps, peg rails – everything is at eye height to draw your interest upward.
Black and white (above right) The archetypal Scandinavian summerhouse – a charcoal-stained clapperboard exterior with chalk-white detailing.
Inside story (right) Step into the interior, however, and second-hand furniture, bold retro fabrics and quirky folk art combine to create a unique vintage vibe.

Powder blue sets the vintage vibe, helped along with a knicker-drawer palette of talcum-powder pinks, mint greens and gentle lilacs. It's a colour scheme that's feminine, timeless and wonderfully evocative.

The furniture is the epitome of granny chic – that comfortable, nostalgic style that combines blousy floral prints, home sewing and clashing colours to cheerful effect. Loose covers work well here; they add to the thrift aesthetic, but are also deeply practical. The theory with vintage fabrics is the more patterns you mix together the more they harmonize. The cacophony of cushions, covers and window treatments seems to sugest that this is true. Any attempt at coordination would ruin the look.

Pictures and paintings are key ingredients for any vintage scheme. The owners of this summerhouse have taken great delight in hanging a rag-tag assortment of oil paintings, folk art and prints. The arrangements might seem, at first glance, haphazard but there's a guiding principle behind each vignette – putting the landscape paintings together in one group, for example, gives a sense of cohesion to the living room, while choosing to place one large artwork above the wood-burning stove helps create a focal point in the dining space. To get the vintage look right – and stop it descending into fleamarket chaos – you need to stick to some styling basics: creating repetition by neatly stacking things on shelves, for example, or finding design similarities between different objects are just two of the tricks of the trade.

A place to unwind (left) On the veranda, the easy-going vintage theme continues with a painted rocking chair and inviting day bed. Soft pink cotton fabrics, bold stripes and a crumpled linen tablecloth complete the look.

A well-curated collection (opposite, clockwise from top left) A crochet seat cushion and an old school desk add charm to the home office; vintage tins, flasks and crockery complete a beautifully styled kitchen; simple accents in similar colour tones stop the bedroom feeling busy; sweet, witty details and homespun accessories give the space real character.

COLONY GARDEN CABIN

Allotments aren't known for their chic sheds. Unless you live in Norway. In Kristiansand, where garden land is limited, a few lucky residents are members of the local *kolonihager* or colony garden. These exclusive allotments often come with picture-perfect summer sheds – stylish little cabins where you can while away the hours when you're not planting seeds or pulling up potatoes.

The owner of this blossom-bright shed took inspiration from the cheerful perennials that surrounded her in the garden. Contrasting candy pinks and mint greens would have jarred on the walls of a rustic woodland hut, but here, in among the summer flowers, these lollipop shades blend in beautifully. It's a charmingly feminine take on vintage chic. The colour palette is bright but deliberately limited – by sticking to just pinks, reds, whites and greens, the owner has found a way to unify the contents of the shed and create order out of clutter.

Shelves and surfaces are filled to bursting with fifties- and sixties-inspired homewares. From polka-dot carrycases and striped mugs to enamelware and vintage cereal tins, it's a riot of pattern and textures. Gingham tea-towels, floral flasks, summery fabrics and woven baskets hung from the ceiling all add to the sense of domestic nostalgia. The salvaged painted cupboards and a charming set of multicoloured kitchen drawers turn storage into something special. A place for everything and everything in its place.

Natural inspiration (above left) Cutting flowers and bright blossoms inspired the colour scheme for this gardener's retreat.
Keep calm and carry on (left) Mismatched prints and artwork find cohesion thanks to their careful grouping, while a sense of order and neatness brings calm to a visually busy space.
A riot of colour (opposite) At first glance this kitchenette seems chaotically bright. In fact, the palette is cleverly limited to yellows, greens and splashes of red, keeping the decor colourful but contained.

Anyone who sews knows just how tricky it can be to be tidy. From buttons to badges, pins to zips, the flotsam and jetsam of needlecraft can soon engulf a workspace. But storage doesn't have to be dull. In this crafter's cubbyhole, there's been some careful consideration to create a space that's efficient but still inspiring.

The best workshops have practical storage, great lighting and some comfortable seating cleverly woven into a space that's decorated to inspire and fire the imagination. This delightful sewing shed is just that, overflowing with colour, pattern and texture, but also beautifully ordered. From the neatly stacked contents of a vintage glass-fronted cabinet to the delicate wirework shelving, this busy shack is a patchwork of great ideas. Fabric swatches and cut lengths are kept in order thanks to an antique glass cupboard, woven baskets and letter racks. Cotton reels and ribbons are easily accessible in a glass-drawered kitchen unit, while scissors and pens find a home in jam jars and vases dotted around the shed.

Beyond the basics, it's a haberdasher's haven and, ultimately, a celebration of fabric. Cushions, bunting, slip covers, tote bags, upholstery, aprons and tablecloths – no surface is left undressed and no opportunity wasted to bring in bright blasts of pattern and colour. It's a visual and textural treat, with all the warmth and homeliness that you'd expect from a truly inspiring creative shed.

A hive of creativity (opposite) This sewing bee has her equipment, materials and fabric neatly ordered. Vintage accents and fleamarket furniture keep the working environment cheerfully relaxed.
The art of display (above right) A glass-fronted cupboard not only is a practical way to store multiple fabric samples but also gives the colours and patterns a chance to become part of the decor.
All-important storage (right) A simple painted Shaker peg rail is ideal for bags and pinafores – and mini clothes-pegs keep reminders on a chicken-wire memo board.

THE PLAIN & SIMPLE SHED

Unadorned and elegant (opposite) Unfinished pine creates a perfectly pale backdrop for this Plain & Simple Shed. Only the front door is painted green – a deliberate device to draw the eye forward and create the illusion of depth.

Spots of colour (overleaf, left) With a neutral background, splashes of colour will stand out. Here, the pea-green bedding and handful of children's toys provide a welcome contrast to the monochrome timber walls and floors.

Bare beach hut (overleaf, right) The exterior of this seaside retreat is kept deliberately stark to match its minimalist interior. One entire gable end is glazed to make the most of the sea views and flood the interior with natural light.

It's a cliché but less is so often more. The Plain & Simple Shed is an absolute masterclass in understated design and sparse styling. At first glance many of these sheds seem too easy to create; how difficult can it be to have an all-white shed and make it look sophisticated? The answer is very. The Plain & Simple look is trickier to achieve than any other shed style; knowing what to leave out is as hard as knowing what to include. Get it wrong and it looks sterile. Get it right and it's just so enviably chic.

The Plain & Simple Shed

61

It might sound obvious but the starting point is a blank, white canvas. The interior of your shed needs to be white, or at the very least off-white. There's a good reason for this. When you're choosing to decorate a space with very few, or very simple things, the background needs to be as inconspicuous as possible.

In the same way that an art gallery will paint its walls white to force the artwork centre stage, the walls of a Plain & Simple Shed need to create a quiet backdrop onto which you then introduce carefully edited pieces of furniture and accessories. There's also a practical advantage too – light colours tend to enlarge a small space, making even the most diminutive of sheds feel more spacious. As any decorator will tell you, however, there are an almost infinite variety of whites. From the icy-coolness of blue whites to the warmer, yellow-based shades of cream, the choice is up to you, but it's worth bearing in mind that white shades will vary according to how much natural light your shed gets and which directions the windows face. It's not always the case that white will lighten and brighten; get the wrong shade of white and it can feel claustrophobic, unsettling or even depressing.

So, when it comes to decorating your Plain & Simple Shed, consider which way the majority of the glazing faces. If your shed predominately faces south, you're in luck. South-facing rooms are the easiest to decorate, suiting both warm and cool whites (this is because they tend to get plenty of direct, warm sunlight throughout the day). Cool whites – such as those with a blue tinge – will create a crisp, seaside feel, while whites with pink or red undertones impart a warmer, country look. North-facing sheds are more complex and struggle with the fact that they spend all day in shade. Avoid cool whites with a green, blue or grey base and, instead, opt for warming yellow-based whites and creamy neutrals to flood the space with light. East- and west-facing sheds will go from warm to cool, and cool to warm light respectively (in other words they either get the morning sun or the afternoon sun). Depending on when you want to spend time in your shed, think

about which effect you'd most like to amplify with paint. For example, if you have a west-facing room and want to create a warm, cosy environment for the afternoon and early evening, plump for a warm white that will come into its own from midday onwards.

Once your shed interior is painted you can use white fixtures and fittings to play visual tricks and hide areas of the shed you'd rather people didn't see. Storage, shelves, cupboards, waste bins – all of these basic but necessary staples of the shed can be made to 'disappear' into the background with white paint or fabric, enhancing the feeling of size and leaving our attention to focus on other, more eye-catching parts of your outdoor room. Mirrored surfaces will create the same illusion, bouncing light back into your shed and reflecting yet more white.

In the Plain & Simple Shed every non-white piece of furniture and accessory will stand out, so it's important to choose these with care. Anything dark or brightly coloured will immediately draw the eye – a black picture frame, a blood-red chair, a mahogany desk – so use that to your advantage and introduce just a few pieces that really make a statement or focus attention to where it's wanted. For example, a soot-black wood-burning stove will make a glorious focal point in an otherwise white shed, pulling your attention towards the glowing flames and making the

Room to relax (opposite and left) Monochrome interiors can feel cold but this cosy, welcoming sleep space has the ideal blend of a light, bright colour scheme and thick textural accents. Layers of touchy-feely duvets, throws, blankets and towels bring instant comfort and provide a clever counterpoint to the industrial accessories and simple furniture used throughout, including the stylish bathroom.

Beautifully basic (above) The bed is the centrepiece in this indulgent garden retreat and sets the tone for the rest of the decor. Undyed linen, crisp cotton pillows and simple aluminium factory lights blend to create a calming, low-key interior.

soft, cold and warm. Build textural corners or points of interest; heap faux-fur throws and soft cushions of various fabrics onto a battered leather armchair, for example, or pile up a vintage desk with a selection of fabric-covered, cardboard and metal storage boxes. Employing a variety of materials and surfaces will break up monotony in an all-white scheme and add extra layers of interest without compromising the simplicity of the overall look.

Lighting can go in one of two directions. You could go for broke and introduce a statement piece of lighting – a brightly coloured lampstand or a huge chandelier, for example, will create an effective focal point, especially if it's oversized or quirky in its design. With this approach, your lighting becomes a piece of sculpture or ornament in its own right, so let it take centre stage by teaming it with less showy pieces. Alternatively, make your lighting invisible, part of the quiet backdrop. Inconspicuous clip-on spotlights, small white table lamps, plain pendant shades – all these will provide illumination without drawing attention to themselves.

In terms of pattern, keep a tight rein on busy designs and clashing colours. Certain fabrics work effortlessly in Plain & Simple schemes; clean stripes and ticking in neutral shades, for instance, will add interest without being overtly showy. Faded florals and bleached toiles create a timeless, European version of the all-white look, while monochrome geometric patterns or the odd bold print will give a shot of visual energy to an all-white background. In terms of colour, a lot can depend on your location – in northern hemisphere countries, for example, the grey/blue/neutral palette suits the natural light conditions better than brighter, tropical colours.

Textural interest (above) When you are decorating with whites, texture becomes one of the key ways to add interest. Here, the rusted iron table, smooth glass jar, crisp seed heads and ridged wooden walls offer different visual and physical textural accents.

Garden canvas (opposite top) Plain & Simple paint schemes allow the natural elements in your garden to shine through. This muted shed, with its faded grey metal planters, allows the fresh greens and occasional bloom to become the focus of attention.

Sweet harmony (opposite bottom) When you are styling a Plain & Simple shed you need to have the odd object or piece of furniture that catches the eye; this breaks up the uniformity of an all-white scheme and adds a touch of visual zing. Here, the dark cushion, table lamp and tree trunk balance out the all-white decor.

space feel cosy and inviting. Equally, painting your internal window frames black or dark grey will draw your eyes towards the view, creating a wonderful link between the inside of your shed and the garden space outside.

In the Plain & Simple Shed, it's texture that will bring variety and visual interest rather than colour. Soft, warm, fluffy surfaces – in the form of chunky knitted throws or deep-pile rugs – will give your shed a delightful feeling of comfort and homeliness; well-worn textures such as scrubbed pine or distressed paintwork add a sense of character and history; and shiny or hard surfaces will look sleek and effortlessly stylish. Make the most of these qualities in your shed by mixing up contrasting physical textures – rough and smooth, hard and

In the Plain & Simple Shed, anything bright, dark, patterned or unique will stand out. Use this to its best effect, and create quirky focal points and interesting vignettes. These 'accent spots' will also help break up the monotony of large expanses of white.

The Plain & Simple Shed

A visual feast Just because you stick to a limited colour palette doesn't mean you can't pile on the layers, accents and accessories. This gorgeous shed is dressed to perfection with strong sculptural elements, quirky one-off pieces and bags of characterful texture.

ESSENTIALS

SHED STYLE NOTES: **PLAIN & SIMPLE** Create a blank canvas with **whitewash** or off-white paint. Use dark or brightly coloured accents to draw the eye. Layer the **textures** – mix warm and cold, smooth and rough, hard and soft. Keep pattern **plain** or low key – think ticking and faded florals. Create **focal points** with stoves or statement lighting.

KEEP PATTERN TO A MINIMUM. CHOOSE COTTON TICKINGS, PLAIN KNITS AND NEUTRAL LINENS

REFLECTIVE SURFACES ENHANCE DAYLIGHT, PLAY VISUAL GAMES AND CREATE FOCAL POINTS

LIGHT AND TOUGH – THE IDEAL COMPACT SURFACE FOR BOTH INDOORS AND OUT

RUSTIC BUT SIMPLE. KEEP FURNITURE SOLID AND UNFUSSY FOR A CLUTTER-FREE SPACE

PORTABLE PREFAB

Everything about this shed is plain and simple. From its unfussy name – the ÁPH80 – to its back-to-basics design, this remarkable micro-building shows what can happen when architects think outside, or should that be inside, the box.

Because that's what this shed is – a prefabricated box – but one that's so cleverly conceived by Madrid-based architects Ábaton that it takes less than six weeks to make. Fully constructed off site, it arrives where you want it on the back of a lorry, needs only a day to install and provides everything you could possibly desire from a stylish retreat.

At only 27m² (290 square feet), this small space packs a surprisingly large punch, providing an amply sized living room/kitchen, bathroom and a double bedroom all under one roof. The construction is basic – a simple gabled rectangle created from solid timber. Outside, the frame and roof are clad entirely in grey boards formed from wood fibre and cement. The monolithic appearance is deliberate, designed by Ábaton to blend in within a natural setting, like some kind of angular rock outcrop.

From the back it looks, well, undeniably shed-like, but appearances can be deceptive. Take a stroll around the front, open the hinged panels, and you'll discover a garden building that's airy, light and ever so elegant.

Window onto the world (opposite) Hinged grey panels fold back to allow light to pour into the living space of this architect-designed shed. The lack of exterior decor is deliberate – any fussy details would distract from its sleek, monolithic form.

Shed to go (above right) From start to finish design, construction and delivery take just a few weeks. Despite its industrial look, the shed is an object lesson in eco-design, with its pollutant-free materials, sustainable timber and efficient use of resources.

Free from distraction (right) The shed is lined with tightly fitting timber panels made from limed Spanish fir. To keep the interior as plain and unfussy as possible, even the kitchen doors, shelves and fitted furniture are constructed from the same material.

There are lots of architects' tricks at work here, helping to make such a small space feel big. The first is the open gabled ceiling – 3.5m (11 feet) at its peak – which creates a wonderful sense of height. The generous expanse of floor-to-ceiling windows also makes the living space feel open and creates an instant connection with the landscape outside. A lack of fussy details on the interior walls – such as skirting boards or dado rails – stop the eye from being distracted and making the space feel enclosed.

Throughout this portable prefab, whitewashed Spanish fir lines the walls and ceiling, creating a clean but gently textured backdrop and a sense of continuity throughout the space. Everything is millimetre perfect – when you opt for minimalism any mistake is amplified – so computer-controlled cutting machinery is used to make certain each panel fits precisely.

When it comes to decor, restraint is the key word. To keep the interior space feeling balanced and coordinated, all the furnishings, accessories and floor coverings are picked from one place – the Spanish über-cool design brand Batavia. Colour is kept to a minimum. Any shades that do make it inside the space draw subtle reference to the outdoors – skylight blues, wood browns, muddy whites and earthy pinks. The use of natural textures and accents – leather, distressed wood, wool, flowers – also helps soften and humanize the space without compromising any of its glorious directness. It's gorgeous. Plain and simple.

Tucked away (above left) The shelves in the shed are placed unusually high. This serves two important functions; not only does it prevent any objects being accidentally knocked off, but it also draws the eye upwards towards the roof space, adding to the building's generous sense of height.

Petite en-suite (left) It might be small but this cleverly compact bathroom has everything you need, including a washbasin, space for towels and storage baskets. The plain, unframed design of the mirror keeps the wall visually unbroken.

Upwards and outwards (opposite) By opening up the ceiling to its full ridge height and glazing one entire wall, the architect designers have managed to keep the shed's living space from feeling cramped, even when it's dressed with a heavily patterned rug and generous furniture.

URUGUAY BEACH HUT

Heavenly isolation There are few sheds in the world more enviably remote than this. Cabo Polonio, a small fishing village surrounded by vast white sand dunes, lies on the rugged coastline of Uruguay, tucked away from the hustle and bustle of city life.

Kitchen quarters (opposite) There was a lot to squeeze into such a small space, but thinking vertically helped to solve the problem. A mezzanine level was built above the tiny kitchen, providing enough floor area for a generous double bed.

Cabo Polonio is a remote place. Not remote in a 'fifteen minutes' drive from the nearest supermarket' kind of way; we're talking no roads, no electricity, no running water kind of remote. This tiny hamlet in south-eastern Uruguay sits on a peninsula between the Atlantic and a stretch of sand dunes. Here you'll find a smattering of makeshift dwellings. Bohemians and life's escapees have been building their own micro homes since the swinging sixties.

Life is simple. It has to be. Anything you might need has to be carried from the nearest town, 7km (4.3 miles) away, by horse, on foot or, if you're really lucky, using one of the handful of rusty jeeps that occasionally passes by. Residents get their water from nearby wells or by collecting rain water. You have to

really want to live here and, unsurprisingly, many people do, including Gabriela Saludes. Gabriela is fortunate to be the owner of this stylish shack. Having acquired it after years of nagging the original owners, he set out making it into his very own slice of paradise. It's bright, light and sits almost invisibly in its bleached sandy surroundings. His choice of whitewashed wooden floors and walls adds to the coastal feel, and helps keep the space cool on baking summer days. Large windows, fitted with vents, allow fresh air to circulate, while the high gable roof leaves enough room for a mezzanine sleeping space complete with double bed.

The decor is wonderfully plain. Sisal rugs, unfinished timber and undyed linens add earthy tones to the calm backdrop. Any pieces of furniture are carefully chosen – white beanbags and a low table create the perfect relaxed and moveable dining area, while the small bathroom is refreshingly rustic with its bare wood washstand and toilet seat.

Fabrics are few and far between, and shutters remove the need for curtains or blinds. Heavy patterns and strong colours would make this small space feel crowded, but there's also a practical reason for the lack of soft furnishings; the harsh seaside sunlight would fade most fabrics in a matter of weeks. The only dots of colour come from a woven rug and the odd striped cotton throw. Lighting is basic – with no electricity, Gabriela relies on lanterns and candles to illuminate the night.

The kitchen space is a joy. Everything's in miniature – even the gas cooker – giving it the feel of a playhouse cooking area. In such a small setting, every item has to be chosen carefully and stored neatly – the shelves and worktop area are meticulously ordered with just enough equipment to rustle up a quick meal. There's no room for frivolous decor; a long trek across sand dunes must sharpen the mind when it comes to what you bring to your coastal hideaway. And the best plain and simple accessory of all? The unbeatable view out to the Atlantic.

Beach views (above left) With such spectacular scenery it's easy to see why the owner has created so many apertures in such a little building. Curtains or blinds would spoil the effect and even the main door is glazed to take advantage of the Atlantic.

Wood and white (opposite) There's been a deliberate attempt to stick to a rigid palette of white and wood tones, but within these colours there's a rich variety of shades. From the bright cotton whites of the beanbags and the scrubbed beiges of the bathroom to the silvered exterior doors and the soft grey corrugated roof, there's a rainbow of gentle natural tones.

LAKESIDE RETREAT

If you need one room to do multiple things it's vital you follow three rules. First, keep things simple. Second, create distinct areas. And third, learn to be tidy, especially if you want a chic, minimalist retreat. The space in Thomas Sandell's lakeside retreat on the Swedish archipelago is tiny, but nothing is wasted. It also follows the three rules to the letter.

The interior is beautifully austere, just gloss-white walls and no adornments. A lack of pictures and prints can sometimes make a space feel cold and characterless, but here it works. The walls already have visual interest thanks to the tongue-and-groove planks; any more distractions and the space would start to feel enclosed. An all-white colour palette can also feel sterile if it's not broken up with the occasional dab of colour – here, soft throws, bright cushions and the odd pop of zesty red from the window-shutters bring just enough dazzle.

The owner has been careful to create three distinct areas, without the need for physical partitions. The kitchenette, sleeping/sitting area and dining table are clearly defined. It's snug, but there's enough flow between the three separate spaces. To keep things ordered – essential in a Plain & Simple Shed – plenty of thought has been given to storage. A clever pull-out drawer on castors is the perfect place to hide clothes and bed linen under the seating/sleeping area, while the kitchenette has not one but three small cupboards and a narrow shelf to keep ingredients and utensils safely stowed but accessible.

Sit, sleep and eat (opposite) Careful planning and compact, built-in furniture mean this lakeside retreat can provide a functional, comfortable space for every part of the day. The inclusion of a wood-burning stove transforms this basic shed into a comfortable hideaway all year round.

Waterside living (above right) The generous outside seating area is a smart move. If the weather's good, the shed space can spill out onto the veranda and expand the building's potential, almost doubling the available floor space.

Clean and uncluttered (right) Cooking areas are one of the trickiest spaces to get right in a shed. It is essential to keep the area clear, well defined and scrupulously clean. An all-white colour palette adds to the mix.

THE RECYCLED SHED

Witty accents (opposite) The essence of recycled chic is taking something unwanted and reworking it to your own ends. Lateral thinking and a good sense of humour definitely help, as demonstrated by this quirky space full of eye-catching finds and rescued furniture.

Don't overthink it (overleaf, left) In the attempt to create a clever interior we sometimes over-engineer a solution. But often simple is best. The delightful rope-pull handles on this reclaimed timber cupboard show how elegant recycled chic can be.

Mix and match (overleaf, right) Recycled style can often be a heady blend of reclaimed materials and fleamarket finds. In this über-cool shed, salvaged timber creates fabulous fitted storage, while mid-century lighting and accessories provide jolts of intense colour.

We all know the ethical reasons for using recycled materials. But it just so happens that salvage can also create some of the most inspiring and original spaces. Recycled furniture and decor seem to suit outdoor buildings – perhaps it's because sheds, at their core, are no-nonsense places, created from basic materials and often decorated with whatever comes to hand. Whatever the reason, welcome to the Recycled Shed – a place that celebrates being inventive and resourceful and, rather refreshingly, doesn't take itself too seriously.

Shed camouflage (left) Fans of reclaimed materials know just how versatile they can be. One resourceful owner has used salvaged corrugated tin sheets as cladding; the rust adds colour and patination, helping the shed blend into its surroundings.

Building from scratch (opposite) This salvaged shed was constructed from reclaimed timber, much of it still with its original paintwork, and distressed metal sheeting. The effect creates a space that already feels lived-in, aged and loved.

There's no central theme when it comes to salvage chic; it's more about philosophy and practicality than any particular set of colours or accessories. That said, some of the most beautiful and eye-catching examples of the Recycled Shed share certain similarities.

Stylish recyclers take great pleasure in turning one object into another. Repurposing or upcycling can create some really dynamic and attractive pieces of furniture and accessories, many of which would look at home in a cosy shed. Desks created from salvaged planks, coffee tables fashioned from wine crates on castors, ceiling pendants made using old metal jelly moulds – there's fun to be had turning form and function on its head. Skip-rats see potential in everything, from an old oil drum to a redundant window frame, and with a bit of practical magic transform it into chic decor.

To create the look, team these improvised pieces with battered, well-worn chairs and sofas to add comfort and cosiness. There's poignancy in well-loved furniture and accessories – a saggy old armchair represents hours of fabulous idleness, a vintage quilt has warmed numerous knees. There's a proviso here, however. If a sofa looked cheap and garish when it was new, it's only going to look worse with age. Well-worn pieces that work tend to be those that were well designed and well made in the first instance. Like a good wine or a fine antique, only certain things improve with time. Or, to stave off too much scruff, you can mix up recycled furniture with new, shiny pieces to create a nice balance. The rough-hewn, well-chewed look of salvaged furniture and accessories contrasts brilliantly with industrial pieces such as galvanized metal stools or sharply designed office chairs.

In fact, contrast can be the key to creating the Recycled Shed interior. When you put two objects or materials next to each other that are usually seen as opposites, you create exciting results. A rescued Victorian armchair reupholstered in wacky seventies fabric, for example, or a school lectern used as a stand for a book or iPad – you're creating a dialogue between objects, not just placing them around your shed.

Salvage style is also about seeing beauty in objects and materials that don't usually find their way into the domestic arena. Shop, church or industrial fittings, for example, such as enamel lights, school lockers, workshop tables, pews and neon lights look sensational pulled out of context and placed in an outdoor building. Architectural antiques and commercial salvage are often much larger in scale than objects created for the home. Have some fun playing with scale and choosing pieces that dominate your shed or create a real talking point – a vastly oversized mirror, for example, or a huge advertising billboard.

Recycled treasures are often simply but beautifully designed and made from high-quality materials; they improve with age rather than diminish.

The Recycled Shed also celebrates the beauty and potential of all different kinds of materials and surfaces. And whether it's chipboard flooring or a zinc tabletop, there's never any attempt to cover up or disguise what an object is made from. Few things in the salvaged shed are repainted or stained – it's all about appreciating a material's natural, raw appearance, however prosaic.

To prevent your Recycled Shed looking more rubbish-dump than ravishing, however, you'll need to inject a bit of glamour. This can come in the form of small, simple but gorgeous accessories that bring in an element of luxury to counterbalance all that reclamation. Think hand-woven linen tablecloths, soft woollen throws, crisp new glassware or bright enamelware.

For lighting, add an edge with industrial pendant lights or wire light cages. Bulkhead lighting and free-standing tripod spotlights also fit the bill perfectly. (Fluorescent strip lighting, although it's a factory favourite, casts a really unattractive glow, so avoid if possible.) You can temper all these engineering elements with simple fairy lights, small chandeliers, barn stars and paper lanterns. And for recycled lighting, everyone's seen jam jars, tin cans and teacups as candleholders, but a newer, neat trick is to cut off the bottom of an old wine or beer bottle to create a glass shade for a candle, or use a tumbler for a tealight. You'll need a glass bottle cutter (which are available online and at craft stores) and to sand down the cut surface. Look out for bottle-cutting kits such as Kinkajou

or Creator's. A slightly quirkier take on the tin-can idea is to use sardine or mackerel tins – the ones that are oblong in shape, as these can take two or three tealights in a row; some brands, such as La Belle Iloise and Hyacinthe Parmentier, have really cheerful, bright packaging. Or hang small, squat tin cans on their sides, using wire, and pop tealights inside each. You can then suspend these in multiples from the ceiling or hang flat against a wall for a flickering focal point.

Artistic upcycling (opposite) This is the studio of Esther Coombs, an artist who specializes in upcycling. Plates, saucers and wine glasses are combined to make cake stands; broken ceramics become seed markers; and silk scarves are repurposed into cushion covers.

Make do and pretend (above) Ever inventive, Esther drew the fire surround behind her tiny reclaimed stove and decorated the walls with rescued cuckoo clocks, prints and mirrors.

Large scale recycling (overleaf, left) In this vast potting shed, rescued and reclaimed objects are given a new lease of life. Zinc buckets, antique planters and other pieces of vintage gardenalia sit patiently outside, waiting to be put to purpose.

Gardener's delight (overleaf, right) What better way to while away the hours than potting up at a scrubbed-pine table? A wirework bench, old lockers, chandeliers and a zinc-topped table complete the salvaged look.

ESSENTIALS

SHED STYLE NOTES: RECYCLED
Take pleasure in **repurposing** old objects. **Upcycle** redundant materials into chic surfaces and furniture. Learn to love **imperfection** – there's character in the **well-worn**. Mix up the eras. Add visual interest with quirky **commercial** salvage, **school** furniture and edgy **industrial** accessories.

TYPOGRAPHY – QUIRKY, EYE-CATCHING SALVAGE AND AN EASY WAY TO PERSONALIZE YOUR SHED

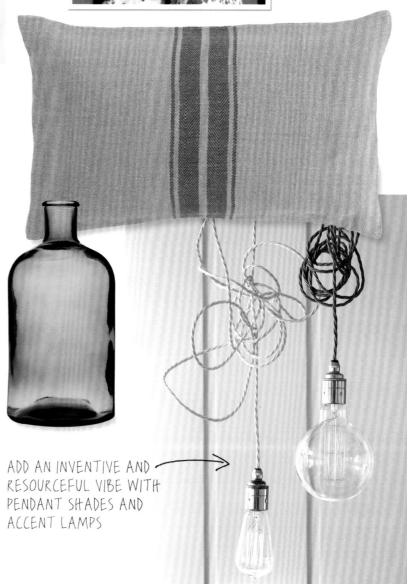

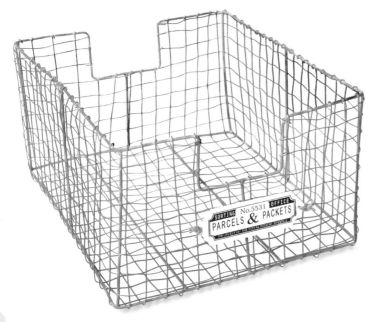

SORTING No.5531 OFFICE
PARCELS & PACKETS

ADD AN INVENTIVE AND RESOURCEFUL VIBE WITH PENDANT SHADES AND ACCENT LAMPS

BOTTLE CRATES – BUILT TO LAST BUT FULL OF VINTAGE CHARM. PLACE ON CASTORS, STACK OR FIX TO THE SHED WALL

FUNCTIONAL, ROBUST AND FULL OF CHILDHOOD MEMORIES, SCHOOL FURNITURE IS DEEPLY PRACTICAL

For illustrator Susi Bramall, life was a bit of a squash and a squeeze. After moving her family of six to a two-bedroom cottage, it soon became clear that she was going to need a shed if she wanted to work from home. Ever resourceful, Susi decided to build her own.

The cottage garden already had some derelict pig buildings. These were quickly demolished, and the sound timbers, windows and corrugated roofing tin were scavenged from the ruins and incorporated into a new oak frame. A chequerboard floor and clean wash of white paint then set the scene onto which Susi could layer her favourite finds, artwork and natural decor.

A roaring wood-burning stove sits at the heart of this delightfully salvaged space. Old pine tables provide useful work surfaces for sewing, drawing and sculpting, while a reclaimed meat cupboard sits next to the fire and houses Susi's paints. A rustic pigeonhole unit, still with its original numbers, now stores scraps of fabric and sewing materials – a particular favourite of Susi's, this functional find was destined for the fire in a carpenter's shop and rescued just in the nick of time.

Small storage is essential for this crafty space. Wicker beakers, enamel buckets, glass jars, vintage tins, old wire baskets, tin cans, wooden crates and confectioners' jars – Susi has thought of so many chic ways to keep her workspace tidy. It seems for this creative spirit, worn, battered and pre-loved pieces are not only the tools of her trade but the very things that inspire her work. Modern just wouldn't cut it.

Favourite things (opposite, clockwise from top left) From old glass jars to canvas seed bags, Susi finds beauty in everyday objects; old reels of twine and vintage medicine bottles create a charming windowsill vignette; an antique pine cupboard with ceramic knobs provides handy wall storage; a stripped kitchen table and vintage folding chair create the ideal sewing area.
Reclaimed accessories (right) Outside, a handful of vintage treasures creates a gentle welcome. A zinc laundry barrel provides handy tool storage and an old garden sieve adds a point of interest on the timber wall.

A scavenger's paradise The urge to rescue is evident in Susi's wonderful workshop. Second-hand furniture rubs shoulders with car-boot finds, pre-loved treasures and hand-me-downs. Even the shed itself was constructed with materials reclaimed from derelict farm buildings.

KARA'S CARAVAN

Caravan kitchenette (opposite) Beach-white tongue-and-groove cupboards provide the perfect surface for Kara Rosalind's collection of rescued goodies. A port-hole window and rope handles complete the coastal feel.

Rich pickings Treasure-hunting trips to European brocante fairs and vintage markets have reaped rewards. From factory lights to antique crockery, it's a cohesive and well-styled collection.

Okay, okay, so this isn't a shed. But it's just so darned lovely it had to earn a place in the Recycled chapter. Not only does this delightful caravan demonstrate what can be achieved in a tiny living space, but it's also packed with armfuls of beautifully chosen brocante.

This 1956 Franklin caravan – known as 'Frankie' – belongs to Australian photographer, stylist and retailer Kara Rosalind. Kara had been working in London, buying and selling vintage wares and salvaged goodies for photo-shoots. Fleamarket chic had already taken hold in Europe, but Kara, realizing there was a gap in the market in her native country, moved back to Brisbane, taking a container-load of old wares and utilitarian pieces with her. She had already honed her treasure-hunting skills at British and French brocante fairs; she was keen to bring the thrill of early-morning bric-a-brac rummaging to Brisbane.

And what better way to follow her potential customers than by selling out of a renovated mid-century caravan. Kara and husband Tim now spend long weekends and holidays on the road, parking up at markets in Queensland and northern New South Wales, and inviting people to pick over their glorious assortment of rescued treasures. This is recycled chic at its most stylish. The caravan was found on the internet, in desperate need of a face-lift. Kara plumped for a coastal theme – painting the outside of the caravan a deliciously blue black and transforming the original bilious green interior with several coats of brilliant white. Navy-and-white striped canvas cushions, rope handles and natural accents completed the look.

What's refreshing is Kara's use of reclaimed treasures. There's a cohesion and unity to her well-curated collection. Stylists know how to take disparate objects and make them work as a whole, and it's clear Kara has an eye for display. Old medicine bottles become a pretty vignette on the edge of a shelf; rusty preserving jars take on a breath of new life filled with tiny white sea shells. Fans of reclamation see the beauty in mundane, practical objects. Kara treats an old garden sieve, shuttlecock and lost feathers as precious ornaments, elevating the everyday into something special.

Other workaday items get reinvented: an old wire shopping basket becomes handy storage, vintage stoneware jars become witty vases, and even an old stepladder becomes a vehicle for display. Galvanized factory lights, English pudding bowls, French wooden spoons, saddles, battered suitcases, glass chemistry beakers – everything in Kara's caravan has beauty and purpose in the right context. There's an enduring quality to many of the objects for sale and perhaps that's the most appealing thing about reclaimed finds. It's no wonder so many of us spend Sunday mornings rooting for recycled riches.

Marine shades (above left) A restricted palette of whites, blues and driftwood browns keeps Kara's caravan from feeling cluttered and adds richness to the vintage seaside theme.

Stylist's tricks (opposite, clockwise from top left) Kara has an eye for display. On this busy shelf, order is achieved through repetition of similar-sized objects and sticking to a monochrome colour scheme; the dazzling striped cushions cut across the stark white interior, adding a welcome splash of colour and pattern; shells, coral, feathers and flowers – nature's bounty provides plenty of free decor; words as art – lost pages from books and vintage postcards add a literary note to the scheme.

THE UPCYCLED INTERIOR

Harry Villiers knows more than most about the potential of recycling. His latest venture, Vintage Archive, sells a vast range of antique and upcycled furniture, vintage posters and graphics, repurposed homewares and art created from recycled objects. He's obsessed with quirky ornaments and objects that have a story to tell. It's perhaps not surprising, then, that his shed should be as eccentric and visually exciting as his collection.

Helped by his sons and a local builder, he constructed his garden retreat from scratch. The building itself is uncomplicated and contemporary – the shed sits on a steel frame (to prevent the need for digging foundations) while the body is constructed from softwood and covered with cedar cladding. A salvaged oval window was donated by a kind friend and, inside, the floor is finished with oak parquet tiles reclaimed from a school.

Like many of Harry's projects, the shed interior is a total one-off. A furniture designer with a background in making props for film and advertising was always going to produce something extraordinary. It's like a cabinet of curiosities meets a theatre props department. Floor-to-ceiling shelves and glass-fronted cupboards are stuffed with curios and one-off artefacts, while the walls are filled with vintage advertisements, maps and antique prints. It's a heady mix of styles but, thanks to Harry's expert eye for form and colour, comes together to create a masculine, intelligent space full of humour and visual wit.

More than meets the eye (above left) From the exterior, you'd guess this was a shed with a sleek, minimalist interior and scant furnishings. Not so. Harry Villiers' treasure trove garden retreat is overflowing with quirky artefacts and upcycled furniture.

A skilful blend (left) Antiques and iconic retro chairs mingle effortlessly with vintage toys, cultural curiosities and cleverly recycled furniture.

Clever contrast (opposite) Painting one wall a contrasting dark colour is an effective visual device. It breaks up the monotony of the pale interior, grounds the space and encourages the eye towards the dramatic oval window.

THE
RETRO
SHED

The queen of mid-century modern (opposite) Orla Kiely's shed is filled to the brim with her signature wallpaper and fabrics; this is 1960s design with a contemporary twist, a clever mix of iconic furniture, bold patterns and collectible gardenalia.

Mid-century minimalism (overleaf) Retro style doesn't have to be a riot of pattern and colour. Just a few key pieces – such as the atomic coat hooks, sheepskin rug and an accent chair – give a flavour of the era without dominating the small space of a shed.

So often retro and vintage style get lumped into the same category. But they are not the same thing. Whereas vintage decor encompasses a wide time span and a heady mix of nostalgic styles, accessories and fabrics, retro is an altogether tighter, more defined look, straight from the middle of the twentieth century and with a very distinctive, bold language of design.

One-room revival (below) From the louvred sliding panels and flat roof to the orange timber-clad walls and ceiling, the entire construction of this garden room draws on mid-century design.

Gently does it (right) The bentwood café chair, white leather pouffe and bright orange telephone scream retro and so they set the tone and colour palette for the rest of the space.

It's an unmistakable aesthetic and one that's often misunderstood. For many people, retro decor is seen as a kind of interior-design joke, a wry smile at the funny furniture and fabrics of the fifties, sixties and seventies. And while there's undoubtedly a playful side to retro interiors, mid-twentieth-century designers produced some of the most ground-breaking and breathtakingly glorious interiors and accessories. From Arne Jacobson's iconic 'egg chairs' to Lucienne Day's dazzling fabrics, retro style still feels as cutting-edge and radical as ever. And,

whether you decide to decorate your shed top to toe or opt for just a hint of mid-century chic, the Retro Shed has to be the coolest hut of them all.

One thing that retro design isn't afraid of is colour. There's no one particular shade that's specifically mid-century; homeowners in the decades that followed World War II had an unprecedented rainbow of colours to choose from thanks to developments in chemical and plastics technology. There are some shades of paint, however, that instantly say 'retro' when you use them – warm oranges, teal, turquoise, lime yellow and garden greens, for example – so it's worth investing in a mid-century heritage shade if you want to get the look just right. Alternatively, you could opt for a Scandinavian-inspired retro palette of cool greys, whites and blues, which creates a sophisticated space and a clean backdrop for eye-catching accessories and furniture.

It's not only the choice of colours but also the way you apply them that will help you nail the retro look. One trick is to paint your shed walls the same colour as any upholstered furniture. This creates a subtle but visually rich effect and will help a small space feel bigger. This type of 'one-colour' interior scheme can be brought to life with black and white accents, which not only help bring some much-needed points of interest but also look exceptionally chic. A different technique, equally authentic for mid-century decorating, is to mix pastel shades and

Forget cheap nostalgia. The mid-century movement was one of the most powerful, refined and forward-looking of all the design eras.

Working with retro This mid-century-inspired study has just the right balance of retro pieces and neutral backdrop. Fifties furniture is often very sculptural – the unusual lines and elegant shapes of this desk really stand out against its plain background.

You can carry the theme of warm wood – teak, walnut, rosewood – from the walls of your shed to the furniture. There are few pieces more iconic than the mid-century wooden sideboard with its tapered legs and gentle curves, so if you can squeeze one into your shed it's an instant way to add retro chic. Mid-century furniture is often very architectural – combining curves, angles and sharp, thin lines – and it's great to soften these striking shapes with thick shagpile rugs and soft cushions. A statement sofa or iconic armchair will create an instant focal point – look out for affordable names such as G Plan, Ercol, Lloyd Loom and Greaves & Thomas, as well as unbranded but equally stylish woven basket chairs, lounge chairs, string garden seats and fifties rocking chairs.

Second-hand modular units will create bags of useful storage – particularly pieces that combine drawers, shelves, cupboards, pigeonholes, desk units, drinks cabinets or other functions. Many of these units are teak or teak veneer and can be picked up on auction sites for a song, especially if you choose late sixties or early seventies models.

You've got some really exciting choices when it comes to fabrics and wallpapers. From modernist motifs and atomic patterns to sixties florals and nature-inspired graphics, you can inject bright sparks of colour and visual zing with retro fabric. Pile on the pattern or add just a small patch in the form of a cushion or chair seat, depending on the look you want to create. Artwork will add another layer of interest – look for reproduction abstract prints, commercial posters and advertisements.

When it comes to accessories, it's not difficult to dig out mid-century ceramics at car-boot sales and charity shops. You can create an instant vignette by collecting differently shaped and sized vases of the same colour – arrange in threes or fives for a 'styled' look. Quirky floor lamps, table lights, starburst mirrors and clocks, colourball magazine racks and coat hooks, kitsch porcelain and glassware – all add to the rich blend. Don't go for the cluttered look; mid-century chic is fairly unfussy. Stick to a few key pieces, displayed neatly.

Colourful crockery (above) Mid-century egg cups, plates and teacups are plentiful at car-boot sales and charity shops, and provide a cheap and cheerful way to inject instant retro charm.
Rustic retro (opposite) This is a gorgeous, hand-hewn take on mid-century chic. Dazzling retro tiles and bright red/orange accents cleverly weave together with reclaimed timber cupboards, distressed surfaces and practical kitchen pieces.

bright colours. Retro chic is all about contrast, and combining warm and cool colours always hits the right note. Apply strong colours in blocks – one whole wall, for example, or a painted floor to keep the look correct.

Another common theme in retro interiors is the extensive use of timber. Wood panelling was a favourite in the fifties and sixties, and is ideal for a shed interior. Unlike the Rustic Shed, which celebrates roughly textured timber, retro panelling needs to be smooth, finished and more tightly jointed. Colour-wise, think deep, warm cedar tones rather than yellow-pine – you can always use a wood stain to darken your walls. Or, if you want to go Scandi-retro, you could lighten the walls with a liming wax. The direction in which your wood panelling is laid will also affect the feel of the shed; vertical lines draw the eye upwards, making a squat room feel taller, while horizontal lines will add a sense of width.

SHED STYLE NOTES: **RETRO**

Be **bold** with strong colours. Dazzle with **atomic** patterns or **modernist** florals. Create contrast. Look for iconic pieces of furniture and modular units – think curves, angles and sharp, tapering lines. Accessorize with **studio** pottery, **starburst** clocks and **colourball** hooks, but keep things uncluttered.

COLLECTIBLE VASES AND CROCKERY SHOWCASE SOME OF THE BEST DESIGNERS OF THE ERA

ATOMIC FABRICS AND PATTERNS TAP INTO THAT MID-CENTURY OBSESSION WITH SPACE TRAVEL AND SCIENCE

SUNBURST CLOCKS AND MIRRORS –
A PERFECT EXPRESSION OF
THE JOIE DE VIVRE OF THE 1950S

ICONIC DOMESTIC PIECES WITH
ARCHITECTURAL LINES, TAPERED
LEGS AND SLENDER CURVES

A Victorian railway carriage by the sea. It's not an obvious choice of retreat for the über-cool mid-century brand Mini Moderns. Or is it? Despite initial differences, this is a building perfectly suited to the decor and design ethics of British duo Keith Stephenson and Mark Hampshire.

Unlike many of the other buildings on the beach (which are either passenger carriages or fishing huts), Keith and Mark's shed was originally a guard's van – plonked on the sand during the 1920s for use as a holiday home. Its unusual 'birdcage' roof light floods the carriage with light and this, along with a continuous run of train windows, brings sea views and daylight in spades. To amplify the effect, Keith and Mark painted the entire interior white, creating a bright neutral space to show off their trademark wallpapers, fabrics, cushions, rugs and ceramics.

Original mid-century pieces – both furniture and accents – weave seamlessly into the space, many bought specifically from collectors' fairs or auctions with the guard's van in mind. But at no point do we feel that the space has become a garish copy of the past. There's a restrained hand at work here – only a few select pieces are needed to create the mood. The thin tapered-leg sofa and armchairs make a simple, architectural statement, for example, while collections of studio pottery are reined in by simple shelving. Lighting is low key and understated – from symmetrical bedside lights to elegant lampstands – proving that

Travelling in style (opposite) The birdcage roof light floods Keith and Mark's dining space with coastal light, adding to the airy, uncluttered feel of the space. (above right) The dark carriage exterior provides a welcome counterpoint to the bright, white interior, and lends a Scandinavian note to the building. (right) Authentic retro pieces are placed judiciously for maximum impact – iconic chairs and a sofa blend seamlessly with Mini Moderns' own mid-century inspired accessories.

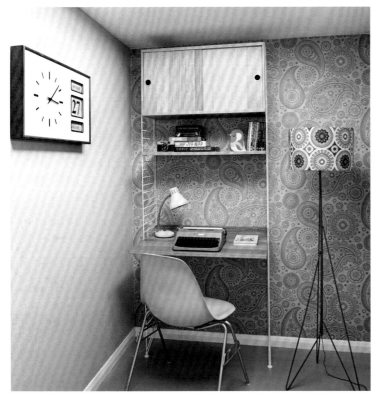

retro doesn't have to be a riot. Even the bucketfuls of bold patterned fabrics and wallpapers create a nice visual tension thanks to Keith and Mark sticking to a similar colour palette in each room – it's a stylist's trick and one that works every time.

The carriage is deeply individual, just like Mini Moderns' take on mid-century style. Its unique homewares and accessories fill the shed, showing off influences as diverse as 1950s textiles, vintage toys and childhood memories. Travel also informs Keith and Mark's work – with much of their inspiration coming from holidays and field trips, both at home and abroad. How apt, then, that their home from home would have taken so many thrilling journeys over the course of its life.

The art of accessorizing (above left) Personal mementos and vintage treasures are carefully curated into neat collections, from a vintage typewriter and office clock to (above right) studio glass and pottery and a Crosley record player. (right) In the bathroom, dark grey and zinc accessories bring coherence, while back in the bedroom (opposite) Keith and Mark's trademark love of atomic patterns and modernist designs is allowed free rein.

Second chances Georgia Wilkinson's 1930s cricket pavilion was rescued and revived by her resourceful farming family. Miraculously, even after a journey on the back of a trailer, it settled nicely into its new surroundings, with all the original doors and windows working perfectly.

A designer's dream (opposite) Georgia's working space is a fabulous reflection of her trademark designs and contemporary furnishings; her passion for textiles, surface pattern and printing blend with a clear retro aesthetic and a strong connection to the countryside.

This is a shed in its second innings. Before fabric designer Georgia Wilkinson rescued it from being chopped up for firewood, this gorgeous 1930s pavilion sat on a cricket pitch only a few miles away. At the end of its useful life the pavilion was sold, lifted onto the back of a tractor-trailer and driven down country lanes to its new home on Georgia's family farm.

For a craftsperson with a sensational eye for colour and pattern, this is the ideal space. Inside, the wood panelling, once dark brown, is now light and bright. Crisp white and turquoise walls provide a perfect backdrop for the retro ceramics, pictures and samples that inspire and inform Georgia's design work.

The layout works perfectly. It's a pavilion of two halves, with changing rooms on either end of the building. Now, as a functioning workshop, this natural separation keeps the 'messy making' – where Georgia creates her lampshades and sews – from the 'clean' clutter-free design side.

It's a skilful mix of modern design and retro touches. The 'Home' and 'Visitors' players' door plaques are lovingly intact, as well as the original storage lockers in one of the changing rooms. These are not only charming but also provide useful, deep storage to keep clutter at bay. In addition, there's ingenious wall-mounted fabric storage, fashioned from old metal guttering brackets, cleaned and spray-painted white – the perfect device for holding rolls of material. Mid-century chairs, covered with Georgia's fabric, and retro coffee pots rub shoulders with modern flat-pack shelving.

Pattern on pattern (left) It takes confidence to layer strong patterns, but Georgia makes it look effortless. Here, rolls of her own retro-inspired fabrics mounted on the wall contrast delightfully with the turquoise owl-covered chair.

Naturally inspired (opposite) Wildlife, birds and floral motifs provide inspiration around the shed and feature heavily in Georgia's fabrics: from hare drawings and a sewing chair covered in bird fabric to stylized flower retro ceramics, ladybird and bee cushions and owl bookends and nature journals.

THE COUNTRY SHED

Potting shed perfection (opposite) Terracotta pots, crate storage, rustic birdhouses and vintage lanterns transform a potting shed corner into a country gardener's retreat; the perfect place to browse through seed catalogues, take tea or simply sit and admire your handiwork.

Tools of the trade (overleaf, left) Country style manages to balance practical elements with pretty finishing touches. Here, rustic gardening basics – trugs, crates, tools and seed trays – harmonize with folk art bird boxes, charming artwork and bright blooms.

Country seat (overleaf, right) Even the simplest of garden structures can have a country twist. A covered bench provides perfect shade from the elements and is softened with sweet decorative accents, including a bucket full of fuchsias, favourite postcards and a simple wreath.

Country is a style that seems impervious to fashion. It's timeless, classic and, above all, unselfconscious, which is perhaps the thing that makes it so appealing. Country Sheds celebrate all things outdoor – gardens, flowers, wildlife, outdoor pursuits – but what differentiates them from Rustic Sheds is that added layer of comfort and luxury.

Rural accents (opposite) Key pieces in this shed bedroom say country chic: gingham and floral fabrics, generous cushions, the Rococo-style chair and bright flower posy lift this rustic setting onto an altogether more luxurious level.

Feminine charms (right) A pretty vignette of a pastel portrait, country print and dressing table trinkets strikes a romantic country note.

Tally ho hut (below right) This child-sized shepherd's hut is filled with riding rosettes and prizes, antique art and horse-related finds – all familiar themes for this miniature country shed.

The Country Shed feels very much an annexe to the house, rather than a complete departure; a place to potter rather than hunker down for days on end. It's this gentleness and accessibility that are so endearing. What could be nicer than settling down in an old chair with your favourite walking book, flask of hot tea within reach and a woollen blanket to keep away the chills: total bliss.

In terms of decoration, country is a style that covers many different looks. From château chic, with its distressed furniture and pretty linens, to the English rose interior, full of cheerful blooms, powder whites and pink fabrics, country style can encompass a wide range of schemes – modern, cottage, French, shabby chic, classic, gardener's retreats and many more. There are, however, similarities between these different interpretations: a love of antiques (whether plain or painted), the generous use of fabrics, profusions of botanical and wildlife motifs, and a love of nature's found accessories – feathers, twigs, driftwood, antlers, shells and other *objets trouvés*.

Country interiors interpret rural life through rose-tinted glasses. And why not? It's a romantic style, one that takes the best of pastoral living and celebrates it. When you're thinking of decorating your shed, certain objects say country more than others. A scrubbed-pine table, floral- or tartan-covered armchair, paintings of flora and fauna, bunches of hand-tied wildflowers – these are some of the unmistakable signifiers of country style. But beyond that, it's down to personal interpretation.

Rugged country, for example, is a style that's taken hold recently and particularly suits the shed aesthetic. The cosy internal space of a hut is ideally suited to the dark, rich tartans and hunting memorabilia that characterize this traditional but timeless look. From the heather purples and leaf browns to spruce greens, the colour palette of rugged country is rich and seasonally inspired. Reds and burnt oranges work well too – shades of autumn leaves and winter berries.

Bare timber walls create the perfect backdrop for club armchairs, sporting accessories and the odd well-chosen antique, while flooring tends to be practical but visually warm – think reclaimed timber planks peppered with rugs or thick sisal matting and sheepskin rugs. For furniture, battered leather or corduroy is not only hard-wearing but it's cosy too – an oversized armchair creates the perfect retreat for one; see if you can find space for a side table as the perfect prop for a post-yomp snifter. Or, if you're planning to have a sociable shed, a

Lunch alfresco (below) A well-loved deckchair, distressed bistro table and rustic café chair provide an informal, relaxed setting for a lazy outdoor meal, protected from the midday sun by a simple suspended linen shade.

Painter's paradise (opposite) An artist's retreat takes a subtle approach to country style, keeping the space uncluttered but cosy. A floral cushion, country dining chair and trio of frames provide touches of rural decor without being distracting.

well-worn sofa teamed with footstools creates a companionable arrangement. Foldaway chairs such as three-legged fishing stools and camping chairs accommodate extra bottoms when needed.

Don't be afraid to layer on the blankets, cushions and throws; a multitude of textures always adds warmth and interest. Rich tartans and checks are the obvious choice for chic lodges and can be used for carpets and wall coverings as well as soft furnishings, tablecloths and throws. Contrasting tartans will harmonize, so don't be afraid to go mad with plaid – the strong lines and grid-like designs of tartan offset any colour differences. You can also take inspiration from other country-wear fabrics, such as tweed and herringbone weaves, sporting and animal pictorial prints, waxed cottons and quilted fabrics. Faux fur and hides will add another level of plush comfort, without the guilt, and can be used on floors, walls or furniture to add interest and softness.

When it comes to accessories, the paraphernalia of country pursuits creates delightful decorative accents – fishing nets and rods, vintage leather cartridge bags, walking and shooting sticks, canoes and oars, snowshoes and old wooden skis – and really adds to the outdoor feel. Vintage sporting prints, sepia photographs and old maps never look out of place either. Small framed pictures with a similar theme – say hunting dogs or wildfowl – look sensational grouped together in an informal but elegant arrangement.

If all this rural styling is a little too traditional for your taste, take a peek at contemporary country. This fresh interiors approach takes familiar symbols of country design – pheasants, ducks, trees, deer – and creates fabrics, wallpapers and accessories with a quirky twist. The colours are lighter and brighter too, from florals in pastel shades to bright linens and voiles. It's an altogether more playful, feminine take on the great outdoors.

Whichever type of country look you go for, keeping snug is essential. If you can find room for a log-burning stove it will bring life and animation to the space. A basket filled with dry wood or a neat stack of logs and kindling is not only practical but also creates its own pleasingly decorative effect. Keep lighting low and intimate – traditional table lamps and brass lampstands create a snug, homely glow, with tealights adding extra flicker.

There are few things more life-affirming than an afternoon of peaceful solitude, surrounded by the paraphernalia of gardening and outdoor living.

Shepherd's rest Gypsy wagons and shepherd's huts
have become the must-have mobile garden accessory,
perfect as home offices, guest accommodation or play
huts. This shepherd's hut, complete with authentic
corrugated cladding and wooden frame, has been
sensitively decorated with bright country fabrics, bold
complementary colours and charming antique furniture.

ESSENTIALS

SHED STYLE NOTES: **COUNTRY**
Look to **nature** for inspiration –
plants, **wildlife** and country motifs.
Blend **practical** surfaces and
furniture with **feminine** touches.
Garden tools, rustic planters and
scrubbed **pine** epitomize the look.
Soften the rural feel with **woven**
blankets, **floral** cushions and a
comfy, battered **armchair**.

SHOP FOR RECLAIMED PLANTERS,
OLD GARDEN TOOLS AND QUIRKY
OUTDOOR ACCESSORIES

ART AND ILLUSTRATION
WITH A NATURE
THEME ADD INSTANT
COUNTRYSIDE APPEAL

A WOODEN PAINTED CHAIR FROM THE HEART OF THE HOME. SOFTEN WITH A SCUFFED CUSHION

AN OLD ARMCHAIR. BATTERED LEATHER, FADED ROSES OR RICH TARTANS – FIND A FABRIC THAT SUITS YOUR SCHEME

GARDENER'S DELIGHT

Country Sheds encapsulate what many of us long for in our lives: a quiet space, surrounded by the sights and sounds of nature, but comfortable and homely in the same breath.

This glorious garden room belongs to Sandra Nilsson and epitomizes the rural idyll complete with mix-and-match chairs, a snug day bed and country accessories. Cushions piled high, touches of floral art and feminine fabrics – this is the perfect space to escape to if the hurly-burly of city living gets too much. It's about rustic simplicity, home comforts and that all-important connection to outdoor living.

Country style runs right through the bones of this shed. Natural, robust materials take centre stage – tough floorboards, scrubbed -pine surfaces and a plant-inspired colour palette. Mossy and leaf greens provide most of the colour in this relaxing space, broken only by the odd sky-blue accent or busy flower print. The floor grabs the eye instantly – a clever trompe l'oeil of old boards painted to look like chequerboard tiles – and adds a strong interior-design note to an otherwise functional space.

It's a haven, one that blends the need for practicality with quirky country decor. Rural furniture and rustic storage are key to this look – so much of the vocabulary of country chic is here: apple crates, antique quilts, naive floral artwork, old pine tables, painted dining chairs, stepladders, peg rails, plant pots, country cupboards, woven rugs and wicker baskets.

Country Sheds like this are such restorative places. Contact with the garden and natural world are absolutely key to wellbeing and relaxation. It's perhaps telling that when most people imagine their perfect home they don't picture themselves in the living room or bedroom, but instead create a mental picture of themselves sitting, overlooking the garden, sipping a glass of wine and enjoying the surroundings.

Rural reclamation This gorgeous glazed garden room was constructed from old windows and doors discovered at a local fleamarket; to create a unified space, the lush green-and-white colour scheme was carried from the walls and woodwork down to the chequerboard floor.

But perhaps most of all, there's a sense that this is a place for family life and cordial gatherings. It's a welcoming space, one that invites you to stay, share food and talk. Country Sheds should be informal, relaxed and perhaps, just that little bit scuffed. The furniture and decor should help you to feel comfortable rather than constrained, at ease rather than on your best behaviour. Somewhere where you can kick off your wellies, put your feet up and watch the sun slip over the horizon.

Blurring the boundaries (above left and above) Delicate country touches – butterfly motifs, floral paintings and living plants – create a subtle link between the interior space and outside in the garden.
A sociable space (left) The room was designed to be a family retreat, a place to relax, enjoy the view and share meals surrounded by fragrant herbs and flowers gleaned from the garden.
Sweet dreams (opposite) In a corner of this calming retreat, an antique iron bed provides the perfect spot for a postprandial nap. Cushions and pillows covered in scraps of second-hand floral fabric add a rich helping of retro country.

When you run a successful hotel and interior design business, where do you go to escape? For Jacquie Pern and Peter Silk the answer was on their doorstep – an old timber shed tacked onto their gorgeously rambling eighteenth-century Yorkshire hotel, The Pheasant.

The timber hut was originally the laundry store for guests' towels and linens. Peter, an interior designer known for his relaxed take on rugged country chic, saw the potential and has created a space that not only provides much-needed privacy but also functions as an effective working space.

On a practical level, the old laundry shelves are the ideal storage solution for Peter's magazines, books and tools of the trade – drills, measuring tapes and rolls of fabric. An antique hall table and a balloon-back dining chair create a handsome, relaxed desk arrangement. Small storage is also essential – wicker baskets, leather trugs, garden trays and old suitcases are all filled to bursting. Lighting comes from storm lanterns, a quirky overhead pendant with antlers and a vintage standard lamp.

In the corner of the shed sits a battered but beloved armchair – perfect for coffee breaks and contemplation. An old rug provides colour and comfort underfoot, while generous full-length curtains bring a touch of domestic decadence. Peter's shed is also filled to the brim with old family paintings, French mirrors, antique pieces, swatches, wallpaper samples and quirky finds – each treasured piece bringing character and personality to this quietly refined and creative country hideaway.

Compact country (opposite) Family pieces, antiques and luxurious fabrics bring in a touch of old-school glamour.

Washday essentials (above right) The hotel's vintage linen shelves create ample storage for Peter's work essentials.

The bigger picture (far right) There's a hint of Victorian drawing room about this traditional take on country chic.

HOG HOUSE

It's almost inconceivable that this elegant country shed was once a squealing, chaotic pig barn. The only clue is in its name – Hog House – a playful reference to the building's agricultural past. But there the similarities end.

American interior designer Richard McGeehan has taken an unloved and unlovely pre-war structure in Lake Geneva, Wisconsin, and transformed it into a retreat that artfully blends rustic sensibilities with an urban edge. It manages to walk those difficult lines between minimalist and homely, rural and contemporary, and masculine without the muscle-flexing.

Sheds can often be gloomy spaces but not here; an unbroken run of large casement windows stretches the entire side of the building, allowing Richard to enjoy glorious views of the open landscape while flooding the space with light. Whitewashed timber cladding – laid horizontally – runs throughout the 13.5m (44-feet) structure, providing a clean but visually textured backdrop onto which Richard has placed a carefully edited selection of simple furnishings, characterful artworks and elegant vintage accessories. It takes an experienced eye to mix antiques with salvage, fleamarket finds with French paintings, but the Shaker-like simplicity of the shed provides the perfect blank canvas for this sophisticated take on country decor. To unite the different spaces, the same colour palette runs throughout – greens, greys and soft yellows – used sparingly but absolutely essential to lift an otherwise monochromic scheme and stop the living area, bedroom, kitchen and bathroom feeling squeezed.

Agricultural chic (opposite) Interiors expert and decorator Richard McGeehan transformed this empty pig barn into a covetable country retreat. Never shy of its roots, however, the barn was lovingly painted in a fresh, farming green and named 'Hog House'.

Master bedroom (above right) Richard's harlequin mix of high-end furniture, vintage linens, clean colours and witty salvage creates a stylish but understated version of modern country.

Country bathroom (right) The pale, washed walls are carried throughout the shed space and into the bathroom, creating the ideal canvas for Richard's artworks, quirky finds and simple pieces of country furniture.

SHED DECOR BASICS

Part 2 Now you've been fired up by all those delicious shed styles, let's move on to making it happen. This section covers lots of the different elements that go into creating a useable but comfortable space – from small storage to soft furnishings, wood-fired heating to foldable seating. At the back of the book you'll also find a handy Directory, laid out in different shed styles, listing some of the best places to find products and inspiration to get you out into the garden and creating your very own slice of shed heaven.

WALLS

FLOORING

HEAT & POWER

FABRIC

FURNITURE

STORAGE

APPROACHES TO SHED SPACE

There's no getting around the fact that sheds are inherently small spaces. And while this is a huge part of their charm – the childlike pleasure of a secret den at the bottom of the garden – compact spaces come with their own set of challenges. Conventional wisdom would say that it's vital to make a small space feel bigger, and there are plenty of interior design tricks that will help you create the illusion of space. But there's also an argument for going with the flow and embracing your shed's diminutive proportions. As New York-based designer Roderick N. Shade suggests, 'There really is nothing wrong with a small room... sometimes it's best not to try and make it feel bigger. Just make it the best small room possible.'

In the end, it's down to a mix of practicality and personal preference. If you need a light and airy studio shed, then opening up the space is essential. If you want a cosy hideaway, however, you can break the rules for small-space decorating. Here's a quick guide to both.

Making a small space feel bigger
Maximizing light vs. Creating depth

If you want to open up a small space, one approach is to let in as much light as possible. This can be tricky in a gloomy shed, but there are ways and means. Choosing a white-based colour is an obvious starting point; whites, creams and pale hues will reflect light and maximize the feeling of space. Painting not only the walls but also the ceiling space and floor will undoubtedly help, as will using light-coloured furniture and fittings. Mirrors can add to the illusion of space, but use them judiciously; it can be distracting being surrounded by reflections and confuse rather than conflate the space. If you are lucky enough to have plenty of glazing, and want to maximize light, opt for simple window treatments or none at all – you want to make the most of any daylight.

It might sound counter-intuitive, but using a dark colour in a shed can also create the illusion of space. By using dramatic tones such as midnight blues, inky blacks, deep browns or maroon reds, you play a different visual trick; dark colours give the illusion of depth as they disguise where the walls begin and end, or fade the boundary between wall, floor and ceiling. It's a bold approach to shed interior space, but truly sophisticated and effective if you can compensate for the lack of light with sparkly accents – mirrors, chandeliers, soft accent lighting or a roaring log burner, for instance. Dark colours also provide a sensational backdrop for artwork and collections if you plan to turn your garden hut into a cosy home from home.

Light and bright or dark and handsome Both approaches work in a shed space, depending on the mood you want to create. Deep, sensual colours create a cosy, den-like atmosphere and an exciting backdrop for accessories. White-based tones magnify the sense of space, reflect light, and provide the perfect blank canvas for your favourite furniture and accents.

What to do with your stuff
Clean & simple vs. Creative clutter

Sheds are often our houses in miniature. Whichever approach makes you feel comfortable in your home will also suit your garden hideaway. For many people, knick-knacks and clutter are a distraction they can do without. This is especially true if the shed is going to be an office, where efficiency and organization are key. For others, personal possessions are a source of comfort and homeliness, a must-have if you want to create a cosy hut. Collections, artwork, photographs and life's odds and sods can also be a fillip if you're doing something design-led – a shed filled with inspirational images, swatches or samples, for example, is compulsory for many creative pursuits.

If you do find clutter suffocating it's vital to get organized with your storage; not only will it improve the practical experience of being in your shed, but also fewer visual distractions will help with the feeling of space. Think vertically as well as horizontally – get things hooked on the walls, tidied away on shelves and hanging from the rafters. You can even create a mezzanine level in a substantial shed, perfect for creating extra storage space

or a platform for sleeping. If you prefer things hidden away, benches, boxes on castors and stacking storage will get your essentials out of sight. See Storage, pages 186–201, for more ideas.

Filling your shed with furniture
Supersize vs. Superskinny

It can be tempting to opt for compact, space-saving pieces of furniture in a small shed. The theory is that too many pieces of furniture, or oversized items, will make the space feel cramped. The reality is a little more complex, however, as large pieces of furniture can work well in small spaces, creating a sense of grandeur and comfort, especially if you compensate in other areas. The key is to leave as much clear floor space as possible, so if you want a generous sofa or armchair think of ways to cut down on other pieces that would traditionally sit on the floor – a floor lamp could be swapped for a wall-mounted light, for example, or a coffee table can be switched for a blanket box that also serves as storage. The same applies to desks and tables. Don't scrimp on surface area – be inventive with off-the-floor storage and opt for bookshelves, hanging storage and wall-mounted cupboards instead.

The importance of being efficient Whether you opt for plain and simple chic or a giddy colour palette, shed spaces can soon feel cramped if you let chaos rein. Get to grips with the difference between what you want and what you actually need in your garden retreat. Have less stuff, create plenty of storage and keep it scrupulously tidy.

WALL TREATMENTS

How you decorate the walls of your shed depends entirely on whether it's a heated year-round space or a seasonal, back-to-basics hut. If your outdoor retreat is warm, dry and insulated then you have as many options as a homeowner, from tiles to wallpaper, painted plaster to stretched fabric. For most people, however, their shed is still a seasonal space, designed to be a rustic retreat for the warmer months. With this in mind, any wall treatments need to be tough enough to cope with changes in temperature and humidity, and easy to clean.

WOOD STAINS

It used to be the case that wood stains came in green, brown and little else. Thanks to developments in paint technology you can now get a glorious variety of shed stains and treatments that are specifically designed for use on outdoor timber. Not only will they protect your shed walls from the elements, they also contain strong pigments that won't fade in strong sunlight but still allow the gentle texture of the wood to show through. Stains are easier to apply than traditional paints – thanks to their thinner consistency – and many brands can be spray-applied. Smooth, planed wood obviously takes less paint coverage than rough sawn timber, so that's worth bearing in mind when you are calculating how much stain you'll need. In the past, wood preservatives and varnishes tended to have high levels of polluting volatile organic compounds (VOCs), added to help with the drying process. Look out for newer, low-VOC or water-based products, which are less polluting and create a healthier shed interior.

PAINT

If you want a denser, richer colour, opt for paint rather than a stain. Emulsion is a lovely, chalky product and you can use it on internal timber, but be aware that it's not as robust as paint designed specifically for woodwork and it tends to mark easily. Shed timbers can sometimes leach stains – which will soak through emulsion onto the top coat – and there's the issues of wipeability and resistance to mould. If you can find a little extra in your budget, opt for water-based eggshell instead – it'll give you the same delightfully matt finish but be able to withstand a bit more of a battering. It's also water-resistant, making it ideal for an outdoor building.

A classic shed look is to paint the inside a different colour from the outside; like the lining of an expensive suit, there's nothing better than opening your shed door to reveal that delicious contrast of colours. When it comes to application, however, watch out for paint leaching through slatted woodwork. There's been many a heartbroken sheddie who, on completing the interior of their glorious shed, goes outside only to discover that the paint has dripped through the gaps in the timber boards down the exterior. Do a test area first, go slowly and don't overload your brush or roller. The only other solution is to paint the entire shed – inside and out – with the same exterior paint.

Perfectly painted panelling The sky's the limit when it comes to paints or stains for your shed interior. High-sheen gloss paint will give an instant hint of retro, and a wonderfully robust surface. Eggshell and other matt-finish treatments create a softer, more subtle paint effect and are more forgiving of uneven surfaces.

THE WHITEWASHED LOOK

Outdoor timber is often treated with preservative. This can leave your shed an unappealing shade of orange, so why not transform its interior with a quick wash of colour? Painting rough timber with thick paint can be time-consuming and tricky to get a good finish, so 'whitewashing' is a quick and cost-effective alternative that gives a softer, weathered look.

HOW TO WHITEN YOUR SHED

Thin down water-based eggshell paint with tap water – two parts paint to one part water (you can go for a thinner mix of 50/50 if it's still too thick to apply). Most shed timber is pre-treated so don't worry; you just need the paint for colour, not protection.

Put protective sheets on the floor and mask off any windows – whitewashing can be splashy. Make sure the shed walls are clean, dry and dust-free.

Apply with a large soft-bristled brush, not a roller, in short, even strokes, working into the timber. Don't worry about it being too perfect and even – whitewash should look rustic – but make sure any drips and runs are brushed in.

Repeat until the right depth of colour is achieved, but remember you're not trying to achieve solid colour.

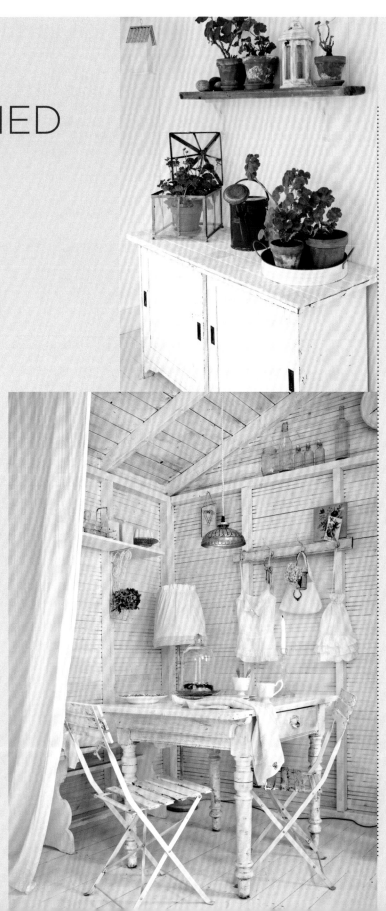

Three ways with whitewash Because whitewash creates a delicate matt finish, it's the perfect treatment for rough timber and distressed furniture. Gloss paint would reflect too much light and highlight all the bumps, cracks and imperfections, whereas whitewash has a smoothing, flattering effect on tired wood and well-loved pieces.

FLOOR FINISHES

Certain factors will affect what kind of floor finish you can have in your shed. The first is how much bounce the floor has in it – this is usually determined by the chunkiness of the floor joists and how close they are together. The second is what kind of material covers the base of your shed to form the floor surface.

Less expensive sheds tend to have narrow floor joists, spaced relatively far apart, and a floor surface created from OSB (oriented strand board) or thin plywood – this is perfectly serviceable for an everyday shed and can be painted, left untreated or carpeted. This kind of floor, however, does naturally have quite a lot of give – not suitable if you want to lay rigid ceramic or stone tiles. If you want a tiled floor you'll need thicker joists, closer together and a substantial floor base underneath, such as 12mm ($\frac{1}{2}$-inch) or 18-mm ($\frac{3}{4}$-inch) plywood.

Some of the more expensive sheds have tongue-and-groove floorboards, which are lovely waxed, varnished or painted. If you go for the last option, always use floor paint – it dries faster, resists marking and copes with abrasion better than normal paint. Plywood can also look

surprisingly chic varnished – either high-gloss or matt – or lightened with lime wax.

Vinyl and linoleum are easy-to-clean, hard-wearing options and an instant way to add a splash of colour to your shed floor. Vinyl is cheap, cheerful and practical, but hasn't got great eco-credentials as it's made from petrochemicals; lino, on the other hand, is entirely natural (made from linseed oil, wood flour, resin and limestone powder), hard-wearing but costlier.

Low-cost, robust flooring
Life for a shed floor can be tough. Only the most luxurious of retreats will need carpets so stick to tough, inexpensive finishes and coverings instead. From scrubbed, bare timber to painted floorboards, you can bring in pattern and colour with trompe l'oeil patterns or artistic flourishes.

SALVAGED FLOORING

If you want to add character to your shed in an instant, create a floor from salvaged materials. It makes sense ecologically, but more than that you get all the patina, colour and back story of a material that's had a previous life.

Costs can vary wildly; if money's no object, reclaimed oak floorboards – the wider the better – will add well-worn, antique charm in spades. Mid-price, you can buy gloriously pink-hued redwood and old-growth pine floorboards (often made from salvaged mill beams), which will only improve with wear and time. The wider the boards, or the longer the complete lengths, the more expensive they'll be.

As a general rule, the more work the material needs the cheaper it will be to acquire. Reclaimed floorboards that require de-nailing and either planing or sanding will be cheaper than ready-to-fit boards that require no clean-up work on your part. Salvaged parquet flooring is also surprisingly inexpensive to buy; the blocks often need cleaning of their old bitumen floor adhesive (a long-winded job) and re-laying carefully.

If you've got the skill and patience, however, it can look sensational.

For the inventive salvage hunter, other reclaimed materials can create excellent flooring. Aluminium floor panels – mostly used in commercial and industrial settings – will create a non-slip, super-chic shed floor that can withstand even the most chaotic of creative pursuits. Go skip-ratting for second-hand builder's materials such as discarded bricks (but always ask the owner first). Old scaffolding planks, pallets and crates are often dumped and can be dismantled for their timber – any stains, knocks and lettering will only add to their rustic appeal.

The art of reinvention Reclaimed materials can be put to an entirely new purpose. Salvaged wall bricks and pavers can be put to use on your shed floor, while timber of all description is easily re-sanded and reused. Laying materials in a decorative pattern – such as a herringbone or brick bond design – adds another level of visual texture to the surface.

RUGS & CARPETS

Hard floors are undoubtedly practical, but there's nothing nicer than softness underfoot. It can be a challenge to combine cosiness and practicality and, for unheated sheds, there are certain floor fibres more up to the job than others.

Coir, sisal, jute and seagrass make excellent natural choices and create an easy, neutral background for any style of shed interior. All cope with heavy domestic use and are durable and hard-wearing. They'll also withstand changes in temperature and humidity, but may need an extra level of stain protection if you plan to subject them to endless muddy wellies. If you want a rug that can withstand the elements, there's a flooring material designed to look like natural flooring but has all the durability of woven vinyl. Made from polypropylene, it's not an eco-friendly option, but is so robust and waterproof that it can even cope with being left outside.

Wool and cotton rugs are luxurious choices, perfect if you want to create a sleepy hideaway or extra living quarters. They're also a bit more vulnerable, so are suitable only if your shed space is insulated and damp-free, or you can drag them back indoors when the weather gets cold. One of the joys of shed decor is that you can often use pieces that might be too threadbare for the house but still have enough wear for your garden hideaway. A vintage rug, for example, will add bags of personality and you won't have to sweat about stains. For petite sheds, small cotton flat-woven rugs or bathmats are super affordable, come in a wide variety of colours and have the benefit of being machine-washable.

Comfort underfoot Rugs bring a much-needed touch of cosiness to hard flooring. Opt for resilient materials that will withstand the inevitable wear and garden dirt; seagrass squares, simple flat-woven cotton mats and second-hand runners are all perfect, low-cost ideas and designed for areas of high traffic.

HEATING & INSULATION

One of the biggest challenges is keeping a shed warm and cosy. By their very nature sheds are temporary buildings, designed for practicality rather than comfort. With a bit of tweaking, however, most garden buildings can be padded out to keep in the heat and create a year-round space.

Sheds lose heat from all sides – the roof, walls and floor will need to be insulated if you want to stay toasty. The easiest way is to line your shed interior with sheets of rigid insulation (look out for names such as Kingspan or Celotex), which don't take up much depth and are foil-covered to help repel moisture.

It's a job for a competent DIYer or tradesman – and you'll find instructions at any large DIY store or online – but the layers should be as follows: shed wall, rigid insulation, vapour barrier and final internal finish (i.e. plasterboard, tongue-and-groove or MDF panelling). As a general rule, go for as thick insulation as you can accommodate – 50mm (2 inch) or more if possible. The lower the u-value the better, as this is an indicator of how much

heat you'll stop from escaping. Heat will also be lost through any sections of glass, so if it's in your budget opt for double-glazed windows and doors if possible. Failing that, think about interlined curtains/blinds or secondary glazing to keep things snug. Once things are insulated, rugs or matting (see previous pages) will keep you warm underfoot, while portable heaters or oil radiators will soon take the chill from the space. For the ultimate shed space, however, you could always think about a wood-burning stove.

WOOD-BURNING STOVES

Wood-burning stoves are an indulgent and fabulous addition to any shed, creating a irresistible focal point and a means to transform a cold hut into a year-round cosy space. They're also a relatively

eco-friendly form of heating – wood is considered a carbon-neutral fuel as the amount given off when it's burning is balanced out by the carbon a tree absorbs when growing.

There are, however, some fundamentals in terms of fire safety and building regulations. Sheds don't usually need planning permission (although this depends on their size, position and use), but you still need to follow any local government regulations set out for heat-producing appliances.

Issues such as carbon monoxide poisoning, smoke control, ventilation and fire prevention are as important

in your hut as they are for your home. It is absolutely essential that you get any wood-burning stove installed by a registered fitter; not only will they be able to help you calculate how big a stove you'll need and where to site it, they'll also know how to fireproof any surrounding walls, create a non-combustible hearth, install a flue that draws properly and create adequate ventilation.

When you're buying a wood-burning stove it's always wise to go for the smallest kW output recommended for the room size – you'd be surprised by how much heat even the smallest model can kick out, especially once the body

of the stove has reached its optimum temperature. Stoves designed for small craft such as canal boats or shepherd's huts are absolutely ideal for the smaller shed and won't leave you gasping for air. Vintage wood burners can be charming, but get a registered installer to check they're safe to use. If in doubt, buy new; modern wood burners are not only more efficient, costing you less to run in the long term, but have also been rigorously safety-tested.

Once you're up and running, get the stove pipe professionally swept at least once a year to prevent a build-up of soot. Burning wet logs is the biggest culprit when it comes to causing soot build-up, so make sure you stick to well-seasoned logs and store them somewhere dry.

Wood is good Nothing beats the gentle crackle of a real wood fire. Stoves that burn well-seasoned timber are an ideal option for sheds and better for the environment than oil- or gas-fired alternatives.

LIGHTS & POWER

If you can get light and power to your shed, they will transform the space from a temporary hut to a useable extra room for living, sleeping and working. Getting a power supply outside, however, comes with a safety warning. Water and electricity are a potentially fatal combination, so it's vital you get any outside electrical work done by a qualified tradesman.

In most instances getting a mains power supply to a shed is straightforward and will involve spurring an extra supply from your home and burying the cable in a trench under the garden.

It is possible to simply snake a cable along the surface of the garden, but most countries' building regulations prefer it to be hidden out of harm's way. If you do decide to sink a cable along the garden, it's often recommended that you go below ground at least 1m (3 feet) and lay warning tape above the cable to prevent overzealous gardeners digging too near.

Running a normal extension cable from the house into the shed is extremely dangerous. Any cables that are outside need to be armoured – this isn't just to protect the wires from water, but also stops rodents nibbling away or you digging through the cable by accident. With a mains power supply your shed can be heated, cooled, lit and set up for technology – providing a real home from home or fully functioning workspace.

If you don't need constant power or don't want to go to the expense of providing the shed with its own mains power supply, you can always opt for the sun-powered route. You can now buy solar kits that include a photovoltaic panel light enough to fit on your shed roof. One kit should provide enough juice to illuminate your shed for anything up to 18 hours – ideal for pottering about long after the sun's gone down.

Getting connected Leaps and bounds in modern technology mean it's easy to stay connected when you're squirreled away in the shed. It's relatively inexpensive to get mains power and a telephone line down to your garden retreat but, if that doesn't appeal, WiFi technology, longer battery lives and solar power often mean you don't even have to stay plugged into the grid.

FIXED LIGHTING

As with any interior scheme, lighting is key to the ambience and enjoyment of your shed. Task lighting will be absolutely essential if you want to use your shed for creative pursuits or desk work; its purpose is to illuminate the specific area or thing you want to work on.

The most effective task lamps are those with manoeuvrability, so you can focus the light exactly where you need it. Look for adjustable-reach arms, tilt and swivel heads, flexible goosenecks or clip-on bases. Practical task lighting isn't always pretty, however, so if it's in your budget look for lamps inspired by icons such as the Anglepoise or Arne Jacobsen desk light, or modern classics like Philippe Starck's elegant D'E light.

General lighting comes into its own when you want to find something in your shed, or you've just stepped over the threshold and need to get your bearings. Presuming you've got mains power, there are some gorgeous pendants, from retro fabric shades to wonderfully camp chandeliers, and everything in between. Aluminium pendant factory-style lights, rice-paper shades

and plastic ceiling globes will create the look for little cost, but if ceiling height is an issue, consider wall-mounted bulkheads or flush-fitting ceiling lights. An elegant solution – combining task and general lighting in one – is a low-voltage wire system onto which you attach multiple LED spotlights exactly where you need illumination.

Ambient lighting will always add to the mood of a space. From flickering candlelight to elegant uprights, these sources of light will help you create cosy corners and glittering effects. Have fun bringing a hint of the domestic interior to your outdoor shed with table lights, lampstands, candelabra and fairy lights. Nothing beats the feeling of being snuggled up on a favourite armchair with a gripping read in hand, table lamp glowing away gently at your side.

Light ideas You'll need to think about illumination if you want to use your shed after hours. There's a myriad of options depending on task and type; from enamel factory pendants and quirky industrial-style pieces to sparkling vintage chandeliers and strings of welcoming fairy lights.

PORTABLE LIGHTING

Portable lighting comes in many different forms – some visually pleasing, others purely functional. It is decorative as well as practical.

SOLAR

Small solar-powered lamps and lanterns sit on the windowsill or veranda of your shed, capturing sunlight during the day, to release a gentle ambient glow during the evening. Solar fairy lights and nets will also add real sparkle to the shed's exterior walls and can be draped around to suit the occasion.

FLAME

Candlelight provides a gorgeous companionable flicker and is the perfect portable lighting for shed entertaining and garden parties. Covered candlelight is best for a timber shed – storm lanterns, jam jars and tealight holders are ideal and safer than bare candlesticks. A favourite of happy campers everywhere, butane/propane lamps also provide powerful carry-around lighting on demand.

WIND-UP

Operated by a dynamo, wind-up lights are another renewable source of portable lighting. As well as torches, look for wind-up lanterns A minute's winding usually gives around half an hour of light – and won't cost you a penny in electricity.

BATTERIES

Battery-powered LED sparkly lights and nightlights come in some delightful shapes – from bunnies to toadstools – and will add touches of playful illumination around your shed. For close-up tasks and gentle ambient lighting, battery-operated LED lamps are an easy option if you haven't got mains power. You can get everything from clip-on book lights and floor lamps to desk lanterns and pull-cord table lamps.

Get carried away You can inject real glamour and intimacy with candlelight and other forms of portable lighting. From simple tealights in antique shot glasses to carved squashes and storm lanterns, these small bursts of light add instant atmosphere and a comforting flicker.

HOW TO CREATE CANDLELIGHT HOLDERS

Old metal cheese graters make gorgeous candlelight covers – the tiny holes let the candlelight flicker through.

Espresso cups are the perfect size for tealights – group in odd numbers or in rows.

Hang vintage ladles from your shed walls and place a tealight in each for instant wall sconces.

Carved-out mini squashes make pretty candleholders – look for dwarf varieties such as Pattypan and Honey Bear.

Use garden wire to fix terracotta thumb pots to your shed wall – ideal for gentle illumination.

Metal paint tester pots – cleaned, labels on and with a tealight hidden inside – look sensational in a neat row and create an uplighter effect.

FABRIC

Fabric can do so many things. It brings warmth and comfort to hard surfaces, darkness and privacy and, best of all, it offers endless ways to inject colour, pattern and visual texture to your shed interior. Fabric can take you in so many directions. From the natural, rough beauty of rustic hessian and linen to the delightful ditziness of floral cottons and vintage chintz, the choices are rich and varied.

If your shed is dry and insulated you'll have every fabric at your disposal. UV bleaching can be an issue, however, so stick to lightfast material for curtains and blinds. If the space is subject to changes in temperature and humidity, consider some of the fabulous new water-resistant fabrics now available. Designed for outdoor cushions and upholstery, these gorgeous materials are often moisture-resistant, colour-fast and washable – perfect for any outdoor room.

Think about budget-busting ways to source great fabric for your shed. Roll ends are always good value – you can pick them up at wholesale manufacturers for a fraction of their retail price. Seconds are also a bargain, the 'mistakes' in the fabric often negligible. Second-hand curtains and clothes – gleaned from fleamarkets or charity shops – offer a treasure trove of vintage patterns and colours for cushions and seat covers, while contract or industrial fabrics can provide some really chic raw materials.

Linen tea towels or flour sacks, for example, make stylishly rustic cushion covers, while agricultural hessian can create inspirational curtaining.

HOW TO MIX FABRIC PATTERNS

Vintage style revels in clashing pattern, but for most other shed interiors there needs to be an element of harmony. Here are four fabric formulas guaranteed to help:

Pattern + pattern + pattern – Blend three striking patterns in the same shed, but stick to one unifying colour.

Pattern + solid + neutral – Choose one pattern. Mix with fabric in one coordinating solid colour and one neutral shade, i.e. white cotton or linen.

Pattern + pattern + neutral – Choose one large pattern, one smaller-scale pattern (with the same colours) and one neutral fabric.

Cheat – Opt for a branded fabric range with its own set of matching pattern fabrics.

Find a common thread You can have some real fun with fabrics; they are a wonderful way to add colour, pattern and texture to your hut. Just be aware when layering pattern: tartans, florals, stripes and pictorial fabrics can all sit together beautifully so long as they share something in common, usually a colour or a set of colours.

CURTAINS & BLINDS

The addition of curtains or blinds will transform your shed into something much more homely. Not only do they afford a sense of privacy, but also the presence of fabric always softens a utilitarian space, adding a welcome touch of domestic comfort.

If lack of light is an issue, however, there's a balance to be had between letting in as much natural sunshine as possible and the need for some kind of window treatment. In general, keeping curtains simple, unfussy and pulled to the side with tie-backs will stop them over-shadowing your shed. Equally, if you mount roman blinds well above your window frame they'll obscure less of the glazing when pulled up during the daytime.

When it comes to curtains and blinds for outdoor buildings, most fabrics are surprisingly robust – velvet, for example, is fantastically stain-resistant and hard-wearing, while wool is well known for its durability. Cottons and linens can both take being pulled endlessly back and forward, especially those with a high thread count, while blended fibres (such as a silk/cotton blend) will give you a good balance of softness and stability. If you want warmth and privacy, make sure you line any window covering – use thermal interlining or simple polyester wadding. Finish the back of any curtains or blinds with a cotton-based lining that offers UV protection, as this will prevent your precious outer fabric from bleaching.

Delicious drapery Curtains aren't just for windows. You can use drops of fabric to do different things in your shed: from creating a simple room partition, which can be pulled to one side when not in use to open up the space, to providing a generous door curtain or lining an entire hut from floor to ceiling.

HOW TO TIE BACK CURTAINS

A short length of chunky staircase rope will create an instant beach-hut look.

Loosely cinch the waist of your curtains with a pair of old leather belts, perfect for the Country or Rustic Shed.

Strings of mix-and-match beads, button garlands or chunky necklaces will add a pretty, vintage note.

Feather boas, chiffon scarves, antique lace and floral corsages create glamorous boudoir curtain tie-backs.

Bunting, pom-pom garlands or rainbow strips of felt are bright ideas for a child's play shed.

Rough strips of hessian, knotted or tied in loose bows, are simple but elegant, and will complement most shed styles.

Short lengths of chains, chunky knit scarves, fabric measuring tapes, old school ties – think laterally for your salvaged shed.

UPHOLSTERY & SEATING

For shed upholstery and seating, the primary consideration has to be wear and tear. Soft furnishings destined for a garden hideaway will need covers that can withstand heavy domestic use – look for upholstery-grade materials or robust linens.

You can always add touches of luxury – cashmere, silk or mohair, for example – with snuggly-soft throws and strokeable cushions. Fabrics that are traditionally used for work clothing – demins, corduroy, tweeds, leathers, Shetland wool and cotton canvas – also make chic but resilient choices for any shed interior.

Certain projects are a doddle, even for the uninitiated. Re-covering a drop-in chair seat, for example, involves little more than brute force and a staple gun. For other pieces of furniture, if you can't afford to reupholster consider loose covers instead, which have the added advantage of being washable. Or, if you're handy with a crochet hook or knitting needles, you can create chunky knit covers for seats, stools and footrests; ideal if you're going for the vintage vibe.

If crafting isn't your forte, a generous throw and a devil-may-care attitude will get you far. Vintage quilts, picnic blankets and even old rugs can create instant sofa covers. Remember, don't be too worried about creating perfection – the appeal of shed decor is its casual, unaffected nature; cracked leather, the odd rip or stain, mismatched fabrics – it's all part of your shed's rich tapestry. Create anything too pristine and you'll only worry about it getting ruined anyway.

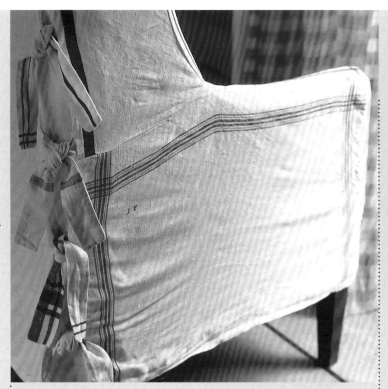

Make do and mend Don't get caught up in creating perfection. Shed upholstery needs to be robust, inexpensive and worry-free. Create armchair covers from scraps of fabric patchworked together, old linen tea towels or roll ends. Drop-in seats are also easy to re-cover – you just need a staple gun, a small length of material and strong hands to pull it taut.

CUSHIONS

Far from being a bit part, the humble scatter cushion has a central role in shed decor. Cushions can perform so many tasks – from adding texture and comfort to bringing together all the different colours in your scheme. It's not always easy to know how many to include, or which colours and fabrics to choose, but some general rules apply:

RULE ONE: Don't go for matchy-matchy fabrics. A scatter cushion sitting on a matching armchair or sofa screams show-home reject.

RULE TWO: Add a variety of textures. Use cushions to bring in feel-appeal. Mix up velvets, linens, faux-fur, chunky knit wool, flannel, leather and other textured fabrics.

RULE THREE: Stick to odd numbers of cushions. Ones, threes and fives create a more lively, dynamic composition, unless you are deliberately trying to create a sense of symmetry on a sofa.

RULE FOUR: Mix up the shapes and sizes. Keep things interesting by introducing a range of shapes – rectangles, circles, squares and bolsters. Vary the size and scale.

RULE FIVE: Cushions aren't just for chairs. They can soften all manner of surfaces and furniture. Don't forget floor cushions, daybed pillows and bench pads.

Scatterbrain No other accessory provides a visual lift more quickly than cushions. They're an instant way to add colour, texture and shape to a shed interior. They're also a great way to use up samples and unwanted scraps of fabric. For the vintage or country look, pile on contrasting colours and floral patterns; for plain & simple or retro, opt for bold, stand-out fabrics and dot them around in odd numbers.

HOW TO EMBELLISH CUSHIONS

For the homespun, crafty look, use embroidery cottons in bright, eye-popping shades to highlight any stitched edges.

Try bobble trims, picot braid and beaded braid to embellish plain linens and hessian for a contemporary country feel.

On wool felt and other no-fray fabric, cut decorative edges using scalloping scissors or pinking shears.

Bias binding is a quick way to cover raw edges and add interest. For a vintage vibe, edge floral fabric with contrasting gingham or polka-dot binding.

Use iron-on no-sew tape or Wonderweb to create instant applique details, or add pocket details using felt or contrasting scraps of fabric.

Use vintage buttons and ribbons to add cute, folksy details or look out for children's iron-patches or embroidered name tags to add a hint of retro school chic.

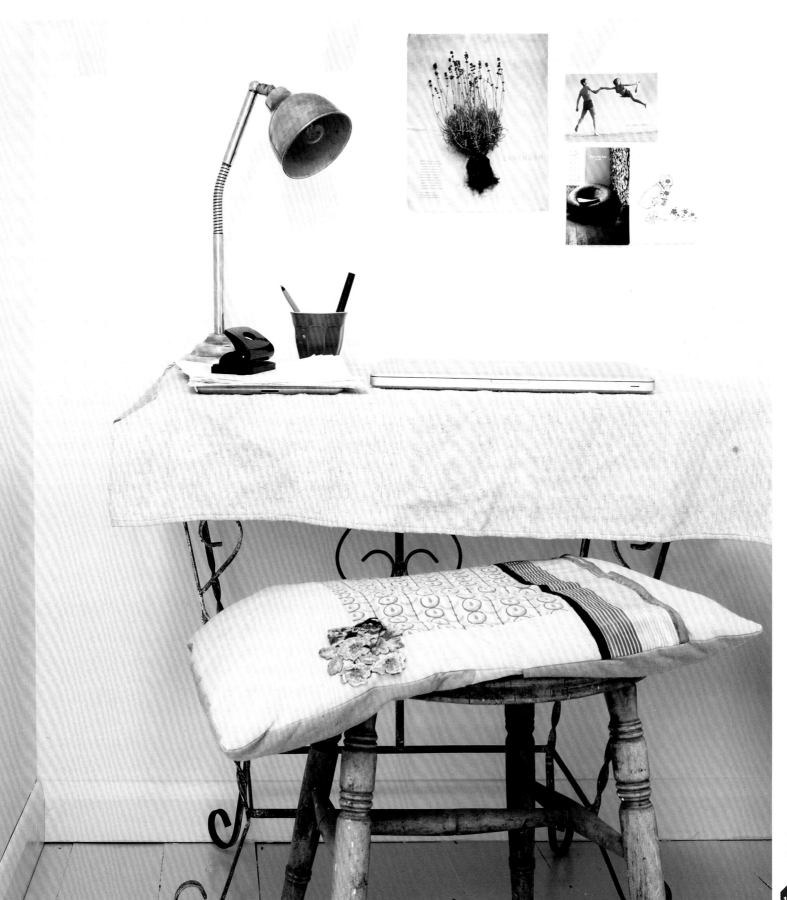

FURNITURE

Shed decor doesn't have to mean outdoor furniture. And while metal café chairs and bistro tables can look wonderfully at home in your garden hideaway, there's also a wealth of kitchen tables, scuffed armchairs, school desks and other domestic delights waiting to be given a new lease of life. Second-hand furniture, vintage pieces and hand-me-downs will all love life at the bottom of your garden and, being already well worn, are perfectly suited to the task in hand.

As long as your shed is dry, most materials can cope with life in an outdoor building. Wooden furniture may swell or shrink depending on the weather and humidity, but as long as you're not storing valuable antiques in your shed, this shouldn't matter too much. The only proviso for wooden furniture is to avoid veneers, which may start to peel in moist conditions. Stick to robust, country pieces, such as planked tables and chapel chairs, if this is an issue.

Painted furniture is ideal for even the most basic of sheds. A good few coats of gloss or eggshell will not only help your furniture cope with the inevitable knocks and scrapes but also add a level

of protection against any damp or UV light, especially if you use exterior-grade paint. It's also an instant and inexpensive way to add pleasing dollops of colour.

Blackboard paint is a revelation if you've never used it before – it's delightfully matt, you can write on it with chalk and it's completely wipeable. Paint an entire wall of your shed and create a huge chalkboard, or use it to give an old chair a glamorous new look. Large pieces of furniture – dining tables, cabinets and linen presses – look amazing painted with this light-absorbing liquid; it has the curious effect of making them seem smaller and yet more dramatic at the same time.

Bring the indoors outdoors
Don't feel restricted to traditional garden furniture. Many domestic pieces will survive life in a garden shed as long as they're either painted, varnished or waxed. Rustic, inexpensive fleamarket finds will withstand the changes in temperature and moisture better than pricey antiques or veneered surfaces.

TABLES & DESKS

One of the best things about furnishing a shed is that you don't have to play by the rules. If you need a table, for example, who says that you have to play it safe and go for a traditional, flat-pack example? Use this opportunity to be inventive, have fun and look to other sources for inspiration. You could create a link between indoors and out by using a foldaway café table that can be tucked away when you don't need it. Design options are varied, from simple pressed steel to slatted wood, but all have the benefit of being light, durable and easy to drag outside if the sun makes an appearance.

For something stout and stocky, look to reclaimed industrial tables – perfect for entertaining large numbers or using as a desk area. Workbenches, architects' drawing boards, canteen tables, wooden trestles, hospital trolleys and other workaday surfaces make truly characterful pieces of furniture; you may have to make a few adjustments to accommodate seating at the correct height, but this usually only involves setting the legs on blocks or taking a little off.

Dressing tables, school desks, butcher's blocks, plant stands, blanket boxes and ping-pong tables – you can adapt lots of different surfaces to your needs. Victorian scrubbed-pine tables are always ready for a tough challenge, as are steel food-preparation benches from commercial kitchens (these make excellent planting tables in a potting shed). For small, occasional tables, steal ideas from interiors magazines: suitcases piled on top of each other, bar stools, upturned crates, reference books

Garden variety Let go of tradition and look for unusual or individual pieces to create a flat working surface. From rough country workbenches to raw timber tables, the rough-hewn textures of pastoral furniture look completely at home in a garden shed.

FURNITURE

piled high, short stepladders, sections of tree trunk, painted oil drums, camping tables, butler's trays, suitcase rests, children's chairs – almost any squat surface can be adapted to suit.

Trestle tables are an excellent option if you want a large-scale but collapsible surface. Trestle legs are lightweight and foldable, making them the perfect solution if you want to hang them on the side of your shed or tuck them out of sight. Any flat surface can become the table-top, from scaffolding planks to an old batten door, but you can also buy ready-made trestle tops in wood, plastic or composite material.

If you want to work on an angled surface, you can also buy adjustable trestle legs that extend with a simple peg-and-hole system. Creating this kind of tilted-top work surface is particularly helpful for close work such as painting, writing or drawing, but it can be laid flat if you want to transform your desk into a dining or display area.

If vintage is your vibe, look out for mid-century camping furniture. Wooden pack-away tables (that fold in half) with matching sets of striped canvas stools, or lacquered metal tables with foldable legs, really capture the look and can be picked up for next to nothing. You can also get

1960s wooden camping tables with printed vinyl tops, often in cheerful psychedelic and atomic patterns – perfect for the Retro Shed.

For large gatherings, German Biergarten tables are great fun. A combination of brightly coloured wooden benches and top, with a tough metal frame, these clever picnic tables can be collapsed when the feasting's over. A quick word of caution, however; many of these vintage tables can be finger-trappers for the unfamiliar, so avoid these if you have small children.

Creative surfaces Second-hand furniture is ideal for shed study and craft. Practically and economically it makes perfect sense, but there's also a visual softness that comes from scuffs, bumps and bangs; nothing beats the appearance of a surface that's grown beautiful with age and use. From architects' chests and kitchen tables to simple trestles and potting benches, the choices are infinite.

SEATING

If space restricts you to one piece of furniture, you can't beat a comfy armchair. A shed should be a space where you can ponder the mysteries of the world, take a quiet moment or just be with your thoughts, and nothing helps this along more than a soft, inviting seat. Traditional wing-back armchairs are a delight and, teamed with a small side table, provide everything a hideaway could need in terms of comfort. If the upholstery is a bit shabby, you can hide a multitude of sins with two large (but flat-ish) cushions, one on top of the seat cushion and one against the inside back.

To take a vintage twist, an armchair can soon be transformed with a blousy chintz or bold pictorial fabric. 'Vintage fabrics' cover everything from pretty sprigs to 1950s nursery prints, psychedelic swirls to gloriously gloomy velvets – and a beautifully re-covered seat or sofa should be the starting point for the rest of your shed decor.

If you want to go retro, low-slung wooden-armed seats scream 'mid-century', especially if you opt for elegant Scandinavian designs. Other style icons from that period include wire-mesh chairs, hanging seats and moulded plastic designs. For plain and simple seating, a leather or linen-covered tub chair makes a quieter statement, while nothing says 'rustic' seating like a chair cobbled together from salvaged timber or a battered old rocker.

Armchairs might not be a practical choice, however, if you want to squeeze in other pieces of furniture. Chapel chairs and church pews are a great choice – not only are they sturdy and pleasingly simple, but also they were

Five ways to put your feet up When choosing a chair for your shed, think about comfort and resilience; an old armchair and sofa are transformed with vintage quilts and crochet, while a rustic timber lounger is instantly softened with a sheepskin. And don't worry about the odd peeling paint or rust patch – this distressed rocking chair and vintage kindergarten seat make a picture-perfect pair.

always designed to provide maximum seating for a limited space. Old cinema seats and school benches work on the same principle, so look out for them at sales and in second-hand shops.

If you want to blur the boundary between indoors and out, certain styles of seat instantly spring to mind. Deckchairs, director's chairs and vintage loungers always make a shed space feel cheerfully 'outdoorsy', but have the added benefit of being foldaway – ideal if you need a flexible floor plan. Garden benches, on the other hand, create the relaxed feel of a 'gardener's rest' – a Lutyens-style wooden seat or slender wirework example, softened with ticking cushions or linen bolsters, is the absolute essence of romantic country decor.

Seating plans Beanbags, director's chairs, bamboo garden loungers and fitted benches – there's an endless variety of seating options if you can't find room for a large armchair. Foldable seats can be safely stored on your shed wall when not in use, while built-in seating will double as a handy storage unit.

HOW TO CREATE SECRET SEATING

Tight spaces make for tricky seating, so it's important to make any chairs, benches and sofas work hard for their place in your shed. Seating that has a dual purpose, or can be hidden away when not in use, is the perfect solution to this perennial problem.

Storage seating – benches and seats that combine wicker baskets or lift-up storage are space-saving must-haves.

Ingenious solutions – from bookcases that transform into chairs and a table, to coffee tables with pull-out seating pads. Look out for new trends in space-saving furniture.

Foldaway furniture – director's chairs, metal garden seating, deckchairs, canvas stools and beach chairs. All are perfect for storing flat on a shed wall.

Light and airy – from sixties-style retro armchairs to blow-up Chesterfield sofas, inflatable furniture is a quick and quirky way to give shed guests a seat.

Built-in for bottoms – take a leaf from caravan design and think of ways to incorporate hinged foldaway seating.

Movable feast – pouffes, beanbags, stacking chairs, leather folding stools, butterfly chairs, ottomans, barrels and fabric cubes all make stylish small-space seating (and in many cases double as side tables and footstools too).

BEDS

It says a great deal that, given the slightest opportunity, many of us happily ditch our home comforts and opt to sleep under the stars. There's clearly something in our DNA that prefers a night spent out in the fresh air, surrounded by pitch-black skies and the gentle sounds of nature. Camping is back on the agenda, but if you don't want rain to spoil your sleepover, you can't beat a bed in a shed.

A space to snooze For most sheds, the inclusion of a sleeping area will take up a good chunk of the floor area. You can approach this dilemma in a few ways. You can reduce the pressure on floor space by opting for bunk beds or a mezzanine level. Or make a virtue of it and turn the bed into the focal point, invitingly complete with cushions, throws and soft pillows.

From sun loungers and foldaway campbeds to vast double beds and shed mezzanines, there's a thousand ways to get a good night's rest. If you need your shed space during daylight hours, think about dual-purpose daybeds and chaises-longues. Roll-up beds, futons and inflatable mattresses are also easy to fold away. Take inspiration from caravan design and think about ways to create hidden sleeping spaces – a bench and table area might reconfigure as a bedbase, for example, or perhaps there's a way to suspend a hammock from your shed walls.

If your garden retreat is specifically designed to be a bedroom, you'll need a more permanent, comfortable arrangement and a good-quality mattress. Think about those all important extras that transform a bedroom into a boutique sleeping space – a cooling fan in summer, bedside tables for books, reading lamps, armfuls of pillows and extra throws. Seclusion is also essential – curtains or blinds are a must, not only for privacy but also to prevent the daybreak from waking your guests.

STORAGE

There's a fundamental conflict between using your shed as a dumping ground and creating an enjoyable extra living space. Such a small building can't cope with both demands, so if you're serious about decorating and using your garden hideaway you'll have to have a purge. Keep only things in your shed that relate to its use – garden tools in a potting shed, for example; brushes and boards in a painter's paradise – and don't let unwanted household items creep in over time.

Regardless of the look you're going for, storage will be essential in such tight surroundings. Even in a gloriously 'cluttered' creative space, there needs to be order underlying the chaos. In fact, it's these busy sheds that need the most effective storage to work efficiently. As with all types of storage, however, it's a bonus if you can find a solution that not only works on a practical level but also adds something to the overall decor. Think pretty glass-fronted cabinets rather than soulless filing systems, personalized boxes over generic plastic containers. In reality, most types of storage can be given a decorative twist: if a filing cabinet is too dull, respray it bright pink; if a cardboard box is bland, cover it in glorious fabric. Even plain shoeboxes can be made more individual with quirky polaroids or handwritten luggage tags.

On a practical level, it's worth thinking about how stored items will fare in your outdoor shed. Open storage is a visual delight but can also be a dust-trap, so consider how much air movement and grime there's likely to be. Shelves and doorless cabinets also require more effort to maintain than a picture-perfect curated 'look', so weigh up whether you're the type of person who enjoys keeping things super-organized or prefers to keep the mess hidden behind closed doors. Often a combination of both works well, keeping most things tucked away with just a few well-chosen or frequently used objects out on show.

Storage with style Storage can be a feature in itself, especially if you find quirky ways to keep clutter at bay. Stacked suitcases not only provide ample space to hide essentials, but also double as a stylish side table, while a three-tier wirework shelf provides an open stage for a vintage crafter's hoard.

CUPBOARDS & CABINETS

Sheds tend to have relatively flimsy walls so, as a general rule, most large cupboards will have to be floor-standing. Vintage glass-fronted cupboards are a delight – the contents become part of your interior scheme. Think of a sewing shed with a cupboard filled to bursting with brightly coloured fabrics and shiny ribbons. There's something special that happens when you display things behind glazing – the contents of the cupboard become more visually arresting, take on more importance somehow. Just make sure that any glass at floor height is safety or toughened glass. If glazing isn't practical or safe, chicken wire is an inexpensive and simple option, and creates an instant rustic French vibe.

Small wardrobes, armoires and kitchen dressers are ideal for larger sheds, and make a space feel wonderfully informal. Don't feel obliged to use them for their original purpose. A battered old kitchen dresser, for example, makes an excellent storage system for craft items – papers and scrapbooks kept neat and flat in the cupboards, and the shelves filled to the brim with pots of brushes, packs of pens and vintage tins full of stationery.

Think about floor space, always tight. An old bedside cupboard, given a new lick of paint, is the perfect pint-sized cabinet for a small shed, as is a narrow school-locker. In a very cramped shed consider how easy it is to access the doors of your cupboard. One large door will need a larger area to swing open than a set of small double doors. If space is really squeezed, doors that concertina or slide sideways are another option, or you can forgo them all together and have open-fronted cupboards.

Up and off the ground, first-aid cabinets, spice cupboards, bathroom cabinets, petite armoires, egg safes and small kitchen cabinets can be fixed securely to the wooden uprights of your shed.

A recycler's dream Upcycled pieces and recycled materials provide a wealth of options for any shed owner. From chicken-wire-fronted cabinets to salvaged lockers, both wooden and metal, these vintage pieces add instant character. Or you can start from scratch and create your own storage using inexpensive reclamation.

REVIVING OLD CABINETS

Decorating your shed is the perfect excuse to give a tired old cupboard a new lease of life. Reclaimed wooden storage will add a lovely note of nostalgia to your outdoor room and provide valuable space to keep your essentials organized.

HOW TO UPDATE AN OLD CUPBOARD

For the Retro Shed, paint your cupboard in an acid shade – bright orange or lime green are perfect. Use a high-gloss paint finish to create that authentic mid-century look. Or cover it with self-adhesive vinyl for a kitsch kitchen look.

To achieve a vintage vibe, paint your cupboard with a heritage eggshell, glaze the cupboard door with safety glass, and line the shelves and back of the cupboard with a chintzy wallpaper (don't use wrapping paper, as it tends to wrinkle when glued).

Old cupboards are often constructed using expensive or scarce woods such as pitch pine or mahogany. For the rustic look, embrace the inherent beauty of these natural woods by removing any layers of paint and finishing with pure beeswax.

For the Plain & Simple look, you can decorate your cupboard a number of ways. Paint in one primary shade or off-black if you want to use the cupboard as a focal point or for display. For functional, invisible storage, paint it the same white shade as the walls, or opt for the limewashed or distressed look.

Interesting infills Most cupboard doors consist of a wooden or glass panel surrounded by timber. Make a feature of this picture-like quality by using a different treatment on the panel from the outside frame. Chicken wire creates an instant French kitchen feel, while a lace infill strikes a pretty vintage note. Mid-century vinyl sticky paper adds a brilliantly retro touch, or you can paint the frame and panel the same colour for a simple, country look.

CRATES & BOXES

Crates and boxes provide plenty of scope for stacking, shelving and sorting. Second-hand and salvaged containers are practical and stylish, perfect for coping with life in an outdoor building but chic enough to enhance any interior scheme. Wine crates and champagne boxes are a popular choice and the staple of any recycled room interior – ideal for floor-standing bookshelves, perhaps set on castors or fixed to the wall in groupings.

Second-life storage All these examples of storage had a previous incarnation. From wine boxes turned into chic drawers to fruit crates as display shelving, the only limit is your imagination. In fact, anything that was designed to be a container can be repurposed into shed storage, whether it's a wicker hamper or a stack of vintage suitcases.

Other sources of reclaimed containers can also make surprising but solid compartments. Vintage suitcases, meat safes, fishing baskets, hampers, metal filing cabinets, bamboo steamers, enamel bread bins, zinc window boxes, old fridge drawers, plastic supermarket delivery crates – there are rich pickings in surprising places for the ingenious shed owner. Dishwasher racks, for example, already come on wheels and can soon be filled with books, magazines or fabric and pushed out of sight under a sofa, sideboard or daybed.

For the resourceful upcycler, single crates and boxes provide the perfect raw material to create new and exciting pieces of furniture. Empty drawers can become individual boxes, while plastic laundry baskets transform into sliding drawers when set onto runners. Even sturdy cardboard boxes can be given a new lease of life painted and lined with a fabric drawstring lining.

HANGING STORAGE

When floor space is at a premium, hanging storage really comes into its own. All sorts of tools, furniture and accessories can be neatly stowed away on the walls of your garden hideaway, from folding deckchairs to scissors and staplers. With safety in mind, be sure that your walls are up to the task. Larch lap panels tend to be too thin to take any weight, so secure heavier pieces from the frame of your shed rather than the panelled walls if you're in doubt.

Hang around It's particularly important to hang up any metal gardening tools away from damp floors and potential damage. An old French shutter with hooks frees up plenty of floor space in this shed, while full-height metal hangers offer an ingenious way to store watering cans. An attractive length of driftwood with hooks creates the perfect place to store your summer panama.

Get hooked Over the years, people have come up with practical and ingenious solutions for hanging storage. Delve into design history and pick a method that suits your style, whether it's Shaker peg rails, Victorian country kitchen shelving or mid-century pegboards and hooks.

HOW TO HANG WITH STYLE

Free up shed floor space with coat hooks, peg rails, clothes rails, pegboards, laundry and pot racks, washing lines and wire hanging baskets.

Look to salvage yards and fleamarkets for quirky ideas – antique cutlery, old garden tools, antlers, vintage taps and reclaimed shoe lasts all make off-the-wall ideas for on-the-wall hooks.

Old sprung bed frames, vintage shutters and propped ladders create extra vertical surfaces to hang things from.

Hanging storage can be creative and constructive. Use hooks to display favourite finds, *objets trouvés*, vintage treasures and eye-catching fabric.

Take inspiration from Shaker-style storage. Hanging chairs, folding furniture and wicker baskets can all be wall-hung when not in use.

Steal ideas from fitted wardrobe companies – canvas pocket storers, hanging shoe racks, clothes tidies and other fabric organizers are all swinging ways to store stuff.

Stationery hangers have multiple small pockets for keeping loose pens and stationery organized. Peg bags and drawstring plimsoll bags are also perfect for small essentials.

SMALL STORAGE

If you're addicted to organization, creating mini storage is the most satisfying task of all. No category of object is too small or item too fiddly to be given its own box, label and dedicated place in your shed. To keep things ordered, think about ways to maintain small storage in a logical system – jam jars can be fixed to the underside of a shelf with a screw through the lid, for example, or unruly plant pots corralled into a high-sided tray.

Cute ways to cache You can run riot with small storage ideas, transforming a cluttered hut into a well-ordered hideaway. From vintage wire post baskets to antique sweet tins, collectible shoe boxes to printer's trays and trusty jam jars – take inspiration from shops, industry and other commercial settings.

HOW TO MAKE MINI STORAGE

Garden delights: take a leaf from gardening, and keep pens, rulers and plant markers in terracotta plant pots, miniature zinc buckets and kids' mini watering cans.

Trash-can treasures: coffee and olive oil tins, baby food and jam jars, aluminium cans, plastic tubs – your recycling box is a great source of free storage fodder.

Kitchen inspiration: Kilner jars, metal cutlery drainers, egg baskets, fruit racks, spice racks, baking tins and mugs – take a cue from culinary storage ideas.

Tools of the trade: steal ideas from the workplace, such as tool boxes, screw draws, printer's type racks, hairdressers' drawers, paint kettles and sweetshop jars.

Chemistry containers: science equipment often doubles as cool storage. Look for test tubes and test-tube holders, glass science beakers and apothecary bottles.

Bathroom beauties: splash out on a few small storage ideas from the bathroom – toothbrush holders, bath caddies, shower tidies and medicine cabinets.

One shed, so much storage

A masterclass in great looks and successful storage, this creative hub effortlessly mingles free-spirited design and meticulous order with the help of some inspired storage ideas, including wicker hampers, glass-fronted cabinets, haberdasher's drawers, vintage letter racks, cardboard filing boxes and confectioner's jars.

DIRECTORY

THE RUSTIC SHED

Best Made
bestmadeco.com
Cool camping and outdoor
accessories, enamelware and
rustic tools

Bodie and Fou
bodieandfou.com
Gorgeous rustic accessories
and inspired ideas

Bowles and Bowles
bowlesandbowles.co.uk
Simple, stripped-back pieces,
including mesh storage racks

Earthborn Paints
earthbornpaints.co.uk
Environmentally friendly paints,
including a water-based wood
stain in eleven shades

Eco Wood Finish
ecowoodfinish.com
Natural wood finishes
including milk paint, eco
varnishes and tung oil

Hen and Hammock
henandhammock.co.uk
Sustainable, eco-friendly
garden products and decor

Le Repère des Belettes
lereperedesbelettes.com
Limited editions, handmade
and rustic-inspired products
from French design duo

Loop the Loop
looptheloop.co.uk
Rustic, chic accessories
for your shed (great for
vintage too)

Rustic White
rusticwhite.co.uk
Natural, earthy and stylish
rustic homewares

Shed
shedtheeclectichome.com
Ecletic rustic homewares,
including sheepskin rugs, faux
fur throws and cow hides

THE VINTAGE SHED

Bazar & Co
bazarandco-store.com
Quirky one-offs, vintage pieces
and eclectic French design

Etsy
etsy.com
Vintage, craft and home-made
furniture and accessories from
around the world

Everything Begins
everythingbegins.com
One-off pieces and vintage-
inspired artwork

Hemingway Design
hemingwaydesign.co.uk
Vintage-inspired wallpapers
and home furnishings from
Wayne Hemingway

Live Laugh Love
livelaughlove.co.uk
Romantic French and British
vintage-style accessories

The Other Duckling
theotherduckling.co.uk
Vintage home accessories,
including knitted textiles and
shabby chic furniture

Rockett St George
rockettstgeorge.co.uk
Eclectic range of homewares
and decorative pieces

Sanderson
sanderson-uk.com
Vintage-, retro- and antique-
inspired fabrics and wallpapers

**School House Electric and
Supply Co**
schoolhouseelectric.com
Chic furniture, lighting and
accessories inspired by
different eras

Woven Ground
wovenground.com
Vintage-inspired rugs – other
styles, too, including shaggy
retro rugs and rustic hides

THE PLAIN & SIMPLE SHED

Design Lemonade
designlemonade.com
Cool homewares based around
a monochromic colour palette

Father Rabbit
fatherrabbit.com
Chic, beautifully designed
treasures and accessories

French Connection
frenchconnection.com
Stylish homewares and
accessories

Huset
huset-shop.com
Scandinavian homewares and
accessories

IKEA
www.ikea.com
Plain, simple, well-designed
furniture and storage

Muji
muji.com / muji.co.uk / muji.eu
Plain and natural homewares,
textiles, stationery and storage

Nordic House
nordichouse.co.uk
Relaxed, Scandi-style
inspiration for your shed

Oyoy
oyoy.dk
Scandinavian style, with
undertones of simple,
Japanese decor

Trunk
trunkhome.co.uk
Unique and beautiful furniture,
textiles, lighting and decor

The White Company
thewhitecompany.com
Stylish, white, high-quality
items for the home

Y10 Store
y10store.com
Elegant, simple accessories
and homewares

THE RECYCLED SHED

Baileys Home & Garden
baileyshome.com
Repurposed, recycled and naturally inspired homewares

Freecycle
freecycle.org
Worldwide network where you can source unwanted furniture and homewares for free

Lassco
lassco.co.uk
One-stop shop for architectural antiques, salvage and curiosities

Nigel's Eco Store
nigelsecostore.com
Practical, functional and beautiful eco-friendly, natural and recycled homewares

Rag Rescue
ragrescue.co.uk
Salvaged French and English vintage fabric and trims. Ships worldwide

RE
re-foundobjects.com
Recycled, restored and rescued homewares and original textiles

SALVO
salvoweb.com
salvo.co.uk
salvo.us
Architectural salvage, antiques and reclaimed building materials

Travelling Wares
kararosenlund.com
Stylish brocante and reclaimed homeware

Vintage Archive
vintagearchive.co.uk
Upcycled furniture, *objets d'art*, original posters, tin signs, toys and graphics

The Yard
thesalvageyard.co.uk
Large and varied stock of reclaimed building materials and architectural antiques

THE RETRO SHED

Anthropologie
anthropologie.eu
anthropologie.com
Retro-inspired wallpaper, accessories and furniture

Elephant & Monkey
elephantandmonkey.co.uk
Original mid-century furniture, textiles and art

Fired Earth
firedearth.com
Kevin McCloud's Mid-Century Colours Collection

Georgia Wilkinson
georgiawilkinson.co.uk
Mid-century-inspired home accessories and fabric

Heals
heals.co.uk
Mid-century-inspired furniture and homewares

Horne
shophorne.com
Modern pieces inspired by mid-century design

Mark Parrish
markparrish.co.uk
Specialist dealer in original mid-century ceramics, lighting, glass and furniture

Mini Moderns
minimoderns.com
Mid-century British-inspired wallpapers, fabrics, cushions, rugs and ceramic.

Orla Kiely
orlakiely.com
Unique retro home accessories and homewares

Show Home
ourshowhome.com
Original retro pieces and contemporary interpretations of mid-century design

THE COUNTRY SHED

Cabbages and Roses
cabbagesandroses.com
Vintage homeware and own-brand fabrics

Fabrics and Papers
fabricsandpapers.com
Designer fabric and wallcoverings, including Kate Forman, Celia Birtwell, Lewis & Wood.

Garden Trading
gardentrading.co.uk
Garden-inspired accessories and lighting for the home and garden

Greyhound Antiques
facebook.com/ pages/Greyhound-Antiques/63405342256
Very affordable antique and vintage furniture and accessories

Ian Mankin
ianmankin.co.uk
Natural and organic tickings, stripes, checks and plains

Laura Ashley
lauraashley.com
Timeless, accessible English country interiors and accessories

The Linen Works
thelinenworks.co.uk
Exquisite raw fabrics, bedding and household linen

Little Greene
littlegreene.com
Luxury paints for outdoor buildings

Peter Silk
petersilk.co.uk
Country-style furnishings and accessories

Maisons du Monde
maisonsdumonde.com
French country chic furniture and home accessories

INDEX

Figures in italics indicate captions

A

Ábaton (architects) 71
advertisements 108
advertising signs *44*, 48, 84
allotments 54
Anglepoise lamps 24, 162
animal hides/skins *16*, *20*, 24, 126
animal horns *20*, *24*
animal prints *43*
antiques 31, 33, 40, 84, *100*, 125, *128*, 137, *137*
antlers *20*, 31, 137, 196
ÁPH80 portable prefab 70–73
appliqué 172
architects' chests 178
architects' drawing boards 176
armchair covers *170*
armoires 188
artwork *10*, *51*, *52*, *54*, 93, 108, *120*, *130*, 133, 139, *139*, 144, 146
atomic patterns 108, 110, *110*, *114*, 178

B

bags
    cartridge 126
    peg 196
    plimsoll 196
    seed *93*
    tote 57
bamboo steamers 192
barrels 182
    laundry *93*
baskets 20, 24, 26, *26*, 54, 57, *72*, 126, 133, 137, 182, 198
    egg 198
    fishing 192
    hanging 196
    laundry 192
Batavia 72
bath caddies 198
bathmats 156
bathrooms *63*, 71, *72*, 76, *76*, 139, *139*
beach carriage 112–115
beach hut 36, 74–77
beakers *93*, 98
beanbags 76, *76*, 182
bed frames 196
bedding *58*

bedrooms/sleeping areas 9, *9*, *24*, *33*, *36*, *43*, *52*, *63*, 71, 76, 79, *114*, *125*, 139, 146, 184, *184*
beds 33, *33*, *63*, *74*, 76, *134*, 184, *184*
bedside lights 113
beeswax 190
benches 28, *28*, 31, *87*, *120*, 146, 172, 176, 182
    potting 178
bias binding 172
bins 24, 63
birdhouses *120*
bitumen floor adhesive 154
blackboard paint 174
blanket boxes 176
blankets *16*, 44, 48, *63*, 125, 126, 130, 170
blinds 158, 168, 184
bobble trims 172
bolsters 182
bookends *118*
books *36*, *98*, 125, 137, 176
bookshelves 146, 182
bottles 31, 87, *93*, 98
bowls *20*, 98
boxes 23, 64, 146, 186, 192, 198
    blanket 176
    filing *201*
    window 192
    wine 192
braids 172
bread bins 192
bricks 154, *154*
buckets 24, *87*, 93, *120*, 198
bunkbeds *184*
bunting 57, 168
butane lamps 164
butchers' blocks 176
buttons 172

C

cabinets 57, 108, 186, 188, *188*, *201*
    medicine 198
    reviving old 190
cake stands *87*
campbeds 184
candelabra 162
candlelight 162, 164
candles 24, 76, 87
candlesticks 31, *31*, 164
cans 87, 93, 198

caravan, Kara's 96–99
carpets 126, *152*, 156
carrycases 54
ceilings 72
    lights 84, 162
    timber *106*
ceramics 108, 113, 118, *118*
chair seats 108, 170, *170*
chairs 44, 63, 84, *102*, *113*, 125
    armchairs 64, 84, 108, 113, 125, 130, *131*, 137, 146, 162, 172, 180, *180*, 182
    basket 108
    beach 182
    bistro 23
    butterfly 182
    café *27*, *106*, *126*, 174
    camping 126
    chapel 180
    children's 178, *180*
    cinema seats 182
    deckchairs *43*, *126*, 182, 194
    dining *126*, 133, 137
    directors 182
    'egg' *106*
    foldaway 126, 182
    folding *93*
    hanging 196
    lounge 108
    loungers *180*, 182
    mix-and-match 133
    office 84
    painted *131*
    retro *100*
    rocking-chairs *52*, 108, 180, *180*
    Rococo-style *125*
    sewing *118*
    stacking 182
    tub 180
chaise-longues 184
chandeliers 44, 48, 64, 87, *87*, 144, 162
cheese graters 164
chemistry containers 198
chicken wire *20*, 188, *188*, 190
child's shed *44*
chintz 166, 180, 190
chopping boards 31
cladding 84, 100, *106*, *128*
clapperboard *51*
clocks *87*, 110, *111*, *114*
clothes rails 196

clothes tidies 196
coat hooks *102*, 108, 196
coir 20, 156
colony garden cabin 54–55
corduroy 170
Cornishware 44
cotton 23, 26, 52, *63*, 68, 156, *156*, 168
cotton canvas 24, 170
country shed 120–139
    essentials 130–131
    gardener's delight 132–135
    Hog House 138–139
    the old laundry 136–137
country style 125, *126*, 133
crate-and-pulley system 33, *33*
crates 23, 24, 26, 34, *34*, *91*, *93*, *120*, 133, 154, 176, 190, 192, *192*
cricket pavilion 116–119
crockery 31, *52*, *97*, *108*, *110*
cupboards 28, 54, 57, *57*, 63, 79, *80*, 93, *93*, *97*, 100, 108, *108*, 133, 146, 188
    updating old 190
curtains 137, 158, 166, 168, 184
cushion covers *87*, 166
cushions *16*, *24*, *33*, 48, *51*, 52, 57, 64, *64*, 98, *98*, 108, 113, *118*, *125*, 126, *126*, 130, *131*, 133, *134*, 166, 172, 180, 182, *184*
    embellishing 172
    seat *52*
cutlery 196
    drainers 198

D

day beds *52*, 133, 172, 184, 192
Day, Lucienne 106
D'E light 162
denims 170
desks *52*, 63, 84, *107*, 108, 146, 176
dining areas 76, *113*
directory 202–203
dishwasher racks 192
distressed pieces 43, *49*, 125, *126*
doors 58, 71, 76, *133*, 190
drawers 54, 79, 108, 192, *192*, 198, *201*
duvets *63*

E

egg cups *108*
egg safes 188
eiderdowns *24*
embroidered name tags 172
enamelware 54, 87
espresso cups 164

F

fabric 166–173
   curtains & blinds 168, *168*
   cushions 172
   mixing fabric patterns 166
   tying back curtains 168
   upholstery & seating 170, *170*
fabric cubes 182
factory lights *63, 97*, 98
fairy lights 162, 164
faux fur 126
feathers 98, *98*
felt 168, 172
firewood *28*
fishing tackle 33, 43, 126
flasks *52*, 54, 125
floor panels, aluminium 154
flooring
   Carrara marble 34
   chequerboard 93, *133*
   chipboard 87
   floor finishes 152, *152*
   linoleum 152
   natural fibre 26
   painted floorboards *152*
   parquet 100, 154
   salvaged 154, *154*
   timber *58, 76*, 125, 133, *152*
   tongue-and-groove 152
   vinyl 152
   see also carpets; rugs
floral fabrics 43, *43*, 52, 64, *125, 134*
flour sacks 166
flowers 54, *54*, 72, *98, 120*, 125, *125, 134*
footstools 126, 170, 182
French château look *44*, 125
fruit racks 198
furniture 174–185
   beds 184–185
   seating 180–183
   tables & desks 176–179
futons 184

G

garden rooms 132–135
garden seats 108, 182
garden sieves *93*, 98
garden tools 34, 130, *130*, 186, 188, *194*
gas cookers 76
gingham 54, *125*, 172
glassware 44, 87, 108, *114*
gypsy wagons *128*

H

hammocks 184
hampers 24, 192, *201*
handles *80, 97*, 98
hangers *194*
heaters, portable 158
heating 158, *158*
herbs 23, *134*
hessian 23, 166, 172
Hog House 138–139
hooks *28, 31, 102*, 110, *194*, 196
hospital trolleys 176
hunting hut 28–31

I

illustrator's studio 92–95
inflatable furniture 182
inflatable mattresses 184
insulation 158
iron-on no-sew tape 172
iron-patches 172

J

Jacobson, Arne 106, 162
jars 57, *64*, 87, 93, *93*, 98, 198, *201*
jute 156

K

kegs *20*
kettles 31, *31*
  paint 198
kilner jars 198
kitchen dressers 188
kitchen units 57
kitchenalia 40, 48, *108*
kitchens/kitchenettes *54, 74*, 76, 79, *97*, 139

L

ladders 33, *33*, 98, 133, 178
lakeside retreat 78–79
lamps 24, *51*, 64, *64*, 90, 108, 126, 137, 146, 162, 164, *164*, 184
lampshades 20, *36*, 64, 118, 162
lampstands 64, 113, 126, 162
lanterns *20*, 24, *24*, 31, 34, *34*, 76, *120*, 164, 164
laundry, the old 136–139
leather 20, 24, 64, 72, 125, 170, 180, 182
LED lamps 164
letter racks 57, *201*
lighting 24, *44, 57, 58*, 64, 68, 76, 80, 84, 87, 113, 126, 137, 144
   fixed 162, *162*
   portable 164, *164*
   and power 160, *160*
   task 164
liming wax 108
linens 20, 23, *23*, 26, 33, *44, 68*, 76, 125, *139*, 168, 170, 172
linoleum 152
living rooms 71, 139
lockers 84, *87*, 118, 188, *188*
log cabins 20, *23*, 28–31
logs 126, 159
loose covers 52

M

magazine racks 108
marble 34
matting 156, *156*, 158
mattresses 184
meat safes 192
memo boards 57
mezzanine levels *43, 74, 76*, 146, 184, *184*
Mini Modern 113, *113*, 114
minimalism 51, *58*, 72, 79, *102*, 139
mirrors *20*, 44, *44*, 48, *51*, 63, *72*, 84, *87*, 108, *111*, 137, 144
modernism 110, *114*
mugs 54, 198

O

objets trouvés 23, 33, 125, 196
offices 9, *52*, 128, 146
OSB (oriented strand board) 152
ottomans 182

P

paint kettles 198
paintings *34*, 44, 52, 125, *134*, 137, 139
paints
   eggshell 148, *148*, 150
   emulsion 148
   gloss *148*
pallets 154
panelling *71*, 108, 118, *148*, 194
pans *31*
pavers *154*
peg bags 196
peg rails 24, 28, *28*, *51, 57*, 133, 196
pegboards 196
pendant lights 24, 87, 162
pendant shades 64, *90*
pews 84, 180
photographs 51, 146
picture frames 63, *126*
pictures 118, 126
pig barn 138–139
pigeonhole units 93, 108
pillows *24, 63, 134*, 172, 184, *184*
plain & simple shed 58–79
   essentials 68–69
   lakeside retreat 78–79
   portable prefab 70–73
   Uruguay beach hut 74–77
plant pots 133
plant stands 176
planters 23, 26, 34, *64*, 87, 130, *130*
plate racks *23*
plates 87, *108*
playrooms 9, 168
plimsoll bags 196
plywood 152
pocket storers 196
polypropylene 156
pom pom garlands 168
porcelain 108
portable prefab 70–73
postcards *98, 120*
posters 44, 108

pot hooks 28
pots
  coffee 118
  plant 133, 198
  storage 24
  terracotta 23, 34, *120*, 164, 198
  tester 164
pottery 110, 113, *114*
potting shed 9, *87*, 120, 176, 188
pouffes *106*, 182
power supply 160, *160*
printer's type racks 198
prints, art 52, *54*, *87*, 108, *118*, *125*,
  126, 133
propane lamps 164

Q

quilts 44, 48, 84, 133, 170, *180*

R

radiators, oil 158
rafters 34, 51, 146
railway carriage 112–115
rattan 24
reading lamps 184
recycled shed 80–101
  beach carriage 112–115
  essentials 90–91, 110–111
  illustrator's studio 92–95
  Kara's caravan 96–99
  retro pavilion 116–119
  the upcycled interior 100–101
retro pavilion 116–119
retro shed 102–119
rooflights 113
roofs 71
  corrugated 76
  flat *106*
rugs *23*, 24, 64, *72*, 76, *102*, 108, 113,
  125, 133, 137, 156, *156*, 158, 170
runners *23*, *156*
rustic shed 16–35
  essentials 26–27
  hunting hut 28–31
  tree house & tool shed 32–35

S

saddles 98
saucers *87*
scaffolding planks 154
Scandi-retro 108
school lecterns 84
sconces *23*, *51*, 164
screw drawers 198
sculpture 44, 64
sea shells 98, *98*
seagrass 156, *156*
seat covers 23
seating 57, 79, *79*, 170, 180
seed markers *87*
sewing shed 56–57
shed decor basic 140–143
shed space, approaches to 144–147
  clean & simple vs. creative clutter
    146
  maximizing light vs. creating
    depth 144
  Supersize vs. Superskinny 146
sheepskins 26, *102*, 125, 180
shelf dividers 23
shelving *34*, 52, 54, 57, *71*, *72*, 76,
  79, *98*, 100, 108, 113, 137, *137*, 146,
  186, 188, 190, 192, *192*, 196
shepherd's hut *43*, *125*, *128*
shoe lasts 196
shoe racks 196
shower tidies 198
shutters *43*, 76, 79, *194*
sideboards 108, 192
sisal 125, 156
sliding panels *106*
slip covers 57
sofas 108, 113, 126, 146, 172, *180*,
  182, 192
solar power 160, *160*, 164
spice racks 198
spoons 98
spotlights 24, 64, 87, 162
squashes 164
Stark, Philippe 162
stationery hangers 196
stools *31*, 84, 170, 176, 182
  fishing 126
  folding 182
storage 23, *23*, 24, *28*, 34, 54, 63,
  72, 79, *80*, 93, *93*, 108, 118, *120*, 133,

146, *146*, 186–201
  crates & boxes 192–193
  cupboards & cabinets 188–189
  hanging storage 194–197
  reviving old cabinets 190–191
  small storage 198–201
studios 9, *87*, 92–95, 144
suitcase rests 178
suitcases *49*, 98, 137, 176, 192, *192*
summerhouse, Danish 50–53
sun loungers 184
sweeping brushes *31*

T

table lights 108, 162
tablecloths 52, 57, 87, 126
tables 31, 44
  bedside 184
  bistro *126*, 174
  café *27*, 176
  camping 178
  canteen 176
  coffee 84, 146, 182
  dining 79
  dressing *125*, 176
  hall *23*, 137
  industrial 176
  kitchen *93*, 178
  low 76
  occasional 176
  pine *23*, *87*, *93*, 125, 133, 176
  ping-pong 176
  side 180, 182
  timber 34, 176
  trestle 178
  workshop 84
  zinc-topped 87
tabletops 87
taps 196
tartans 126
teacups 87, *108*
tealight holders 164
tealights 87, 164, *164*
tea towels 54, 166, *170*
telephones *106*
terracotta 23, 34, *120*, 164, 198
throws 24, 26, *33*, 36, 40, *48*, *63*,
  64, 87, 126, 170, 184, *184*
tiles 100, *108*, 133
timber 23, 31
  bare 20

reclaimed 80, *84*
rough *16*, 24, 26
stained 23
sun-bleached 20
whitewashed *10*, 33
tins 44, *48*, *52*, 54, 87, 198
tongue-and-groove 51, 79, *97*, 152
tool boxes 198
tool shed 34, *34*
toothbrush holders 198
towel hangers *20*
towels 63, *72*
toys 48, 58, *100*, 114
trays 137, 178, 198
tree houses *16*, 33, *33*
tree trunks *64*, 178
trestles 176, 178
trugs *120*, 137
trunks 20
tweeds 170
typography *90*

U

upcycled interior 100–101
upholstery 170, *170*

V

vases 23, 57, 98, 108, *110*
velvet 180
ventilation 158
verandas 52, 79
vintage shed 36–57
  colony garden cabin 54–55
  Danish summerhouse 50–53
  essentials 48–49
  sewing shed 56–57
vinyl 152, 190
volatile organic compounds
(VOCs) 148

W

wallpapers *102*, 108, 113, 114, 137,
  190
walls
  fabric wall coverings 126
  painted 148
  panelled 194
  timber *58*, *64*, *93*, *106*, 125
  tongue-and-groove 51, 79
  whitewashed 76, 150, *150*
  wood stains 148

PICTURE CREDITS

wardrobes 188

washing area *84*

washstands 76

watering cans 23, 34, 198

whitewash *10*, 33, 68, 76, 93, 150, *150*

wicker 24

WiFi technology *160*

wind-up lights 164

window treatments 52

windows 72, 76, *97*, *100*, *133*, 139, 158

wine glasses *87*

Wonderweb 172

wood 20, 23

  distressed 72

  warm 108

  wood stains 148

wood-burning stoves *10*, 26, *28*, 31, 52, 63, 68, *79*, *87*, 93, 126, 158–159, *159*

wools 20, 24, *27*, 72, 156, 170

work surfaces 23, 76

workbenches 176

wreaths 31, *120*

Z

zinc 26, 87, *87*, *93*, 192, 198

Page 1 Alamy; 3 Abaton – www.abaton.es; 4 Jacqui Small LLP / Victoria Harley; 6 top row – left Tom Robertson / Charles Finn – finncharles.wix.com/a-room-of-ones-own; top row – right Jacqui Small LLP / Victoria Harley; middle row – left Harry Villiers / www.villiers.co.uk; middle row – middle Stellan Herner; middle row – right Christine Bauer; bottom row – left Abaton – www.abaton.es; 7 bottom row – right Mini Moderns;t op row – left Jacqui Small LLP / Victoria Harley ; top row – rightJavier Csecs / Styling: Solange Van Dorssen; middle row – right HawthBush Farm – www.hawthbushfarm.co.uk; bottom row – left Kithaus – www.kithaus.com; bottom row – right Alun Callender / Narratives; 8 Camera Press/ MCM/ Yannick Labrousse; 10 Lucas Allen /GMA Images; 11 Lucas Allen /GMA Images; 12–13 Alamy; 15 top row – left Alun Callender / Narratives; top row – middle Holly Joliffetop; top row – right Abaton – www.abaton.es; bottom row – left Jacqui Small LLP / Victoria Harley; bottom row – middle Andrew Boyd / Mini Moderns; bottom row – right Jacqui Small LLP / Victoria Harley; 17 living4media / Annette & Christian; 18 Emma Lee; 19 David Merewether / Constructed by carpenter Rupert Walton; 20 top right Stefano Scata/The Interior Archive; bottom left Jim Hensley / Taverne Agency; 21 living4media / Annette & Christian; 22 EWA Stock; 23 top right EWA Stock; middle Tim Street-Porter / EWA Stock; 24 top middle living4media / Eising Studio; bottom left living4media / Annette & Christian; 25 living4media / Taverne Agency b.v. / J. Hensley & N. Dreyer; 26-27 Alexander & Pearl – www.alexanderandpearl.co.uk Loop the Loop – www.looptheloop.org.uk Toast – www.toast.co.uk Charnwood – www.charnwood.com Anthropologie – www.anthropologie.eu Also Home – www.alsohome.com French Connection – www.frenchconnection.com/ www.frenchconnection.com/homeware John Lewis – www.johnlewis.com Drift Living – www.driftliving.co.uk; 28 Alun Callender / Narratives; 29 Alun Callender / Narratives; 30 Alun Callender / Narratives; 31 Alun Callender / Narratives; 32 Lucas Allen; 33 Lucas Allen; 34 Lucas Allen; 35 Lucas Allen; 37 Holly Joliffe; 38 GAP Interiors/Jake Fitzjones; 39 Brian Harrison / EWA Stock; 40 Anitta Behrendt/Mainstreamimages; 41 Michael Sinclair / Future PLC; 42 Andreas von Einsiedel; 43 Andreas von Einsiedel; 44 top right Ray Main / Mainstreamimages; bottom left GAP Photos/Elke Borkowski; 45 GAP Interiors/Jake Fitzjones; 46 StockFood / Great Stock!; 47 living4media / Steve Lupton; 48 mirror image – Holly Joliffe; 48-49 Mabel And Rose – www.mabelandrose.com Cath Kidston – www.cathkidston.com Oliver Bonas – www.oliverbonas.com Out There Interiors – www.outthereinteriors.com French Connection – www.frenchconnection.com /www.frenchconnection.com/homeware Caravan – www.caravanstyle.com Pale and Interesting – www.paleandinteresting.com The French Bedroom Company – www.frenchbedroomcompany.co.uk An Angel at my table – www.anangelatmytable.com ; 50 Nathalie Krag / taverne agency; 51 Nathalie Krag / taverne agency; 52 Nathalie Krag / taverne agency; 53 Nathalie Krag / taverne agency; 54 Eva Kylland; 55 Eva Kylland; 56 GAP Interiors/Amanda Turner; 57 GAP Interiors/Amanda Turner; 59 Ben Anders; 60 Ben Anders; 61 Ben Anders; 62 Mikkel Vang / taverne agency; 63 Mikkel Vang / taverne agency; 64 Heather Hobhouse for LightLocations.com; 65 Heather Hobhouse for LightLocations.com; 66-67 Petra Bindel; 68 white trestle table image – Polly Wreford / Pale and Interesting – /www.paleandinteresting.com FEBRONIE – www.febronie.com Loop the Loop – www.looptheloop.org.uk House Envy – www.house-envy.co.uk Toast – www.toast.co.uk Sainsburys Home – www.sainsburys.co.uk Bloomingville – www.bloomingville.com French Connection – www.frenchconnection.com / www.frenchconnection.com/homeware ; 70 Abaton – www.abaton.es; 71 Abaton – www.abaton.es; 72 Abaton – www.abaton.es; 73 Abaton – www.abaton.es; 74 Javier Csecs / Styling: Solange Van Dorssen ; 75 Javier Csecs / Styling: Solange Van Dorssen; 76 Javier Csecs / Styling: Solange Van Dorssen; 77 Javier Csecs / Styling: Solange Van Dorssen; 78 Stellan Herner; 79 Stellan Herner; 81 Carina Olander; 82 Carina Olander; 83 Carina Olander; 84 top right Tom Robertson / Charles Finn – finncharles.wix.com/a-room-of-ones-own; 85 GAP Interiors/Mark Bolton 86 Alun Callender / Country Living; 87 Alun Callender / Country Living; 88 Jan Baldwin / Narratives 89 Jan Baldwin / Narratives; 90-91 Dotcomgiftshop – www.dotcomgiftshop.com Alexander & Pearl – www.alexanderandpearl.co.uk Marks and Spencer – www.marksandspencer.com Sainsburys Home – www.sainsburys.co.uk Out There Interiors – www.outthereinteriors.com The Old Cinema – www.theoldcinema.co.uk Dee Puddy Garden and Interiors – www.deepuddy.co.uk Rowen and Wren – www.rowenandwren.co.uk Cox and Cox – www.coxandcox.co.uk; 92 Jacqui Small LLP / Victoria Harley; 93 Jacqui Small LLP / Victoria Harley; 94 Jacqui Small LLP / Victoria Harley; 95 Jacqui Small LLP / Victoria Harley; 96/97 Sharyn Cairns / NewsLifeMedia / Country Style; 98/99 Kara Rosenlund ; 100/101 Harry Villiers / www.villiers.co.uk ; 103 Ros Drinkwater / Alamy; 104 Nathalie Krag / taverne agency; 105 Nathalie Krag / taverne agency; 106 top right Lucas Allen / GMA Images left Kithaus – www.kithaus.com; 107 Elisabeth Aarhus/Mainstreamimages 108/109 Carina Olander; 110-111 teapot image – Jacqui Small LLP / Victoria Harley Hunkydory Home – www.hunkydoryhome.co.uk Magpie – www.magpieline.com Mini Moderns- www.minimoderns.com Berry Red – www.berryred.co.uk Cloudberry Living – www.cloudberryliving.co.uk Alexander & Pearl – www.alexanderandpearl.co.uk House of Fraser – www.houseoffraser.co.uk Marks and Spencer – www.marksandspencer.com Cotswold Trading – www.cotswoldtrading.com Furniture Village – www.furniturevillage.co.uk; 112 Andrew Boyd / Mini Moderns; 113 Andrew Boyd / Mini Moderns exterior shot: Mini Moderns; 114/115 Andrew Boyd / Mini Moderns; 116 –119 Jacqui Small LLP / Victoria Harley; 121 Carina Olander; 122 Trevor Richards / IPC Images 123 Christine Bauer; 124 living4media / Bauer, Christine; 125 top living4media / Bauer, Christine bottom right Jacqui Small LLP / Victoria Harley; 126 Jim Hensley / Taverne Agency; 127 living4media / Elizabeth Whiting & Associates; 128–129 HawthBush Farm – www.hawthbushfarm.co.uk ; 130-131 leather chair images – Atlanta Barlett Sainsburys Home – www.sainsburys.co.uk Out There Interiors – www.outthereinteriors.com Bloomingville – www.bloomingville.com Pale and Interesting – www.paleandinteresting.com Chocolate Creative – www.chocolatecreative.co.uk Cox and Cox – www.coxandcox.co.uk An Angel at my table – www.anangelatmytable.com Rowen and Wren – www.

THANK YOU

SALLY

HELEN

SIAN

CAROLINE

DAD

I'm a lucky girl. There can't be many lovelier ways to earn a living than writing books. As always, huge thanks to everyone at Jacqui Small LLP – Jacqui, Jo, Claire and Lydia – for giving me the opportunity and unswerving support to do what I enjoy. My thanks also to the dream freelance team – Sian, Helen and Caroline – all inspirational women and a hoot to boot. Mum, if you're wondering where Dad is, he's probably in his shed. This book is for you both with all my love.

rowenandwren.co.uk Graham and Green – www.grahamandgreen.co.uk Mabel And Rose – www.mabelandrose.com ; 132–135 Carina Olander; 136–137 Jacqui Small LLP / Victoria Harley ; 138–139 William Waldron /TIA Digital Ltd ; 140-141 Alamy; 143 top row – left Holly Joliffe; top row – middle GAP Interiors top row – right Jacqui Small LLP / Victoria Harley; bottom row – left Jacqui Small LLP / Catherine Gratwicke; bottom row – middle Claire Richardson / Narratives; bottom row – right Jacqui Small LLP / Victoria Harley; 144 Richard Bryant / Ambience Images; 145 GAP Interiors / Tria Giovan; 146 Stuart McIntyre / Ambience Images; 147 Eva Kylland; 148 bottom left GAP Interiors/ Douglas Gibb bottom right Holly Joliffe; 149 Andreas von Einsiedel; 150 top right GAP Interiors/Devis Bionaz; bottom right living4media / Bauer, Christine; 151 Folio Images; 152 top right James Fennell/TIA Digital Ltd middle GAP Interiors/ Johnny Bouchier; bottom right GAP Interiors/Nadia Mackenzie; 153 Carina Olander; 154 top right Sarah Greenman bottom GAP Interiors / Cristina Fiorentini; 155 Carina Olander; 156 top right Anitta Behrendt/Mainstreamimages; bottom Jacqui Small LLP / Victoria Harley; 57 Rachael Smith; 158 GAP Interiors/Robin Stubbert; 159 Jacqui Small LLP / Victoria Harley; 160 Jan Baldwin / Narratives; 161 Brett Charles / IPC Images; 162 top living4media / von Oswald, Yvonne; middle Alexander & Pearl – www.alexanderandpearl.co.uk; bottom GAP Interiors/Colin Poole; 163 Christine Bauer; 164 top Carina Olander bottom Jacqui Small LLP / Victoria Harley; 165 living4media / Bauer, Christine; 166 Claire Richardson / Narratives; 167 living4media / ETSA; 168 IPC Images; 169 Michael Sinclair Jacqui Small LLP / Victoria Harley / The Huts in the Hills – www.thehutsinthehills.co.uk; 170 top right Jacqui Small LLP / Simon Upton; middle GAP Interiors/Amanda Turner; 171 Jacqui Small LLP / Catherine Gratwicke ;172 top GAP Interiors/Jonathan Gooch – Stylist: Charlotte Love; bottom Fritz von der Schulenburg/TIA Digital Ltd 173; GAP Interiors/Rachel Whiting; 174 top living4media / Annette & Christian bottom GAP Interiors/Tria Giovan; 175 Lucas Allen/ GMA Images; 176 Carina Olander; 177 Heather Hobhouse; 178 top Jan Baldwin/Narratives bottom GAP Interiors/Nick Carter; 179 Clive Nicholls; 180 top right living4media / Annette & Christian; bottom right GAP Interiors/Nick Carter; 181 living4media / Bauer, Christine; 182 top right Carina Olander; bottom left Melanie Coles/IPC Images; 183 Holly Joliffe/ Landscape magazine; 184 top right Heather Hobhouse; bottom left Anitta Behrendt/Mainstreamimages; 185 Camera Press/ Avantages/ Christophe Valentin; 186 GAP Interiors/ Amanda Turner; 187 GAP Interiors/Dan Duchars; 188 bottom right Jan Baldwin/Narratives; bottom left Fritz von der Schulenburg/TIA Digital Ltd; 189 GAP Interiors/Rachel Whiting; 190 top right Camera Press/ Picture Press/ Brigitte; bottom left Sonja Bannick; 191 Carina Olander; 192 top right GAP Interiors /Colin Poole; bottom right GAP Interiors /Colin Poole; 193 GAP Interiors/Dan Duchars; 194 top right Jacqui Small LLP / Victoria Harley; bottom left GAP Interiors / Anton Robert ; 195 Petra Bindel ; 196 top left Alexandra Gablewski / Taverne Agency; top right living4media / Lars Ranek; bottom left GAP Interiors/Johnny Bouchier; 97 Michel Arnaud/TIA Digital Ltd; 198 top right Jacqui Small LLP / Victoria Harley; top left Jacqui Small LLP / Victoria Harley; middle GAP Interiors/Mark Scott bottom GAP Photos/BBC Magazines Ltd; 199 Jacqui Small LLP / Victoria Harley; 200 GAP Interiors/ Douglas Gibb